T0370054

TRIUMPH
B O O K S

TOUGH GUYS

TOUGH GUYS

HOCKEY'S ENFORCERS ON WILD BRAWLS, HIGH STAKES, AND THE CODE THAT BINDS THEM

DALE ARNOLD

TRIUMPH
BOOKS

Library of Congress Cataloging-in-Publication Data available upon request.

This book is available in quantity at special discounts for your group or organization. For further information, contact:

Triumph Books LLC
814 North Franklin Street
Chicago, Illinois 60610
(312) 337-0747
www.triumphbooks.com

Printed in U.S.A.
ISBN: 978-1-63727-740-9
Design by Nord Compo
Photos courtesy of Getty Images unless otherwise indicated

CONTENTS

———

FOREWORD

DALE ARNOLD FIRST came to me with the idea of working together to write my autobiography in January 2020. I said no. I didn't think anyone wanted to hear my story, and I didn't think I had anything important to say. I made my bones in the National Hockey League mainly with my fists. It wasn't that I couldn't play the game, but my primary duty was to protect my teammates. My first NHL fight was against a guy named Brad Brown in a preseason game on September 21, 2000, and my last was against Andrew Desjardins on March 25, 2017. That's a long time to do what I did, and I managed to survive 141 fights at the NHL level (and another 84 in the American Hockey League), so I guess I was at least adequate at the position.

It is not a glamorous job, but I would make the argument that it is an honorable one. While the role of National Hockey League enforcer has been diminished over the years, there is still a place for a man willing to drop the mitts and trade a few with someone just as willing. It's an honest day's work for an honest day's pay, and any of us who stepped to the plate did so with full knowledge of what the job entailed and what the consequences could be.

As far as honor is concerned, I have no problem making the case that it is perhaps the biggest part of the job. If you are willing to defend a teammate, no matter what the transgression or the size of the transgressor, that is honorable. I can promise you that no teammate I've ever defended has ever had an issue with me doing it. The role of the NHL tough guy is to allow the more skilled players the room and latitude to do their jobs to the best of their abilities.

Now Dale is back talking with more hockey tough guys. Some I know personally, some I know because of their well-earned reputations, and at least one I've even fought myself (nothing personal, Matthew Barnaby). I know all these guys have some tales to tell!

Hockey has a deep and rich history. All of us who have been lucky enough to have worked in the sport, and those of us who still do, owe a debt of gratitude to those who came before. In every organization I've ever played for, I've had the privilege of getting to know and talk to those who helped build the foundation for our game. I can tell you that one of the highlights of my seven seasons with the Boston Bruins was getting to know the legends of that organization—people like Milt Schmidt, Johnny Bucyk, Bobby Orr, and Terry O'Reilly. There was so much to learn from every one of those great men.

I also think there is much to learn from the men in this book. They all made a living the same way I did, and I respect anyone willing to do that. But they've also lived their own rich hockey lives, and the stories they have to share are important. The stars of our game are provided ample opportunity to share their stories, but that doesn't mean the men featured in the pages of this book are any less important—or any less entertaining.

Because the members of the media spend more time talking to those very worthy stars, reporters naturally have less time to spend with the character players on a team. Maybe that's why when given the opportunity to speak, those guys take full advantage of it. They appreciate that people want to hear them, and they usually find an endearing way to make their voices heard.

I can't wait to hear those voices.

The game is always evolving and will continue to do so. But there will always be a warm place in my heart, and the hearts of many hockey fans, for men known by many names and titles, but with one common thread—they are the *Tough Guys*.

Shawn Thornton played for the Chicago Blackhawks, Anaheim Ducks, Boston Bruins, and Florida Panthers during his 14 seasons in the NHL, winning the Stanley Cup with the Ducks in 2007 and with the Bruins in 2011. He joined the Panthers executive staff following retirement and currently serves as the team's chief revenue officer.

INTRODUCTION

Fellas, Coach McVie sent me out here and asked me to give you a message. He wanted you both to know that if you don't stop running around and taking unnecessary shots at our guys, then both of you are going to the hospital. And I'm gonna be the one who sends you there.

—Archie Henderson, Maine Mariners

THERE IS ONLY ONE SPORT, outside of the combat sports, in which two participants can square off in old-fashioned, bare-knuckle pugilism, serve an appropriate penalty for their transgressions, and then return to the game, perhaps to engage in a second—or even a third—round. In football, baseball, and basketball, players are ejected immediately for fighting. Only hockey has always allowed fighting, perhaps at times even encouraging it.

The sport is not quite what it once was, and there is a segment of fans who wish the game could return to those gory, bloody days of yesterday. Hockey has a place for two willing combatants.

There is even an underground fan base that trades videos of the greatest fights, and there are players who have become legendary not for their prowess with the puck, but for their ability to deliver and receive a punch.

There are great NHL players who also have well-deserved reputations for being able to take care of themselves. But there are also feared and respected NHL enforcers known primarily by nickname. Hockey fight fans know exactly what they can expect from players known as "Bomber," "Biznasty," "The Barbarian," "The Animal," "The Missing Link," "Jethro," "The Grim Reaper," "Bulldog," "Battleship," "Mayday," "Knuckles," "Tiger," and "The Hammer."

Peripheral fans will probably be surprised to learn that people within the game say hockey enforcers tend to be the kindest, gentlest, and most popular players on a team. There are exceptions, but spend any time around some of the most feared players in league history and you'll come away having a hard time believing how they actually made a living. And almost without exception, they are the best storytellers in the game.

This is where I also admit that I am a bad person.

I certainly don't aspire to the Patrice Bergeron "Mr. Perfect" or Nicklas Lidstrom "Perfect Human" level of perfection. Let's not get silly! I only hope to be somewhat right of center on the human evolution timeline—somewhere between *Australopithecus* and *Homo erectus*. I've been married for more than 48 years, so my wife at least puts up with me. My three kids, and their spouses, like to visit. My grandson, Parker, seems to like me—or he is too young to know better. But make no mistake about it: I'm a bad person.

I've never been a fan of blatant and overt violence. I don't ever watch slasher movies. I cringed when Vinko Bogataj suffered the agony of defeat on ABC's *Wide World of Sports*. But I also admit that at certain times, I like to watch human beings hurt other human beings. I enjoy when two men square off in an old-fashioned, bare-knuckle fistfight. I'm not talking about scripted, WWE-like pseudo-violence. I'm talking about real, throw-hands, blood-inducing, knot-lifting, knuckle-scraping violence. The kind that hockey has always offered.

I actually like the fact that there is only one sport that allows two competitors to take out their physical and emotional aggressions, battle like a product of the primordial stew, sit and cool off for a paltry five minutes, and then be allowed to go back into the fray and continue their discourse, if desired. I admit that I like fighting in hockey, and I truly enjoy most of the men who ply that particular way of making a living. I've always found them engaging and interesting.

If you cover the National Football League, as I have, you learn quickly that offensive linemen are the best people to talk to. They have less pretense and far fewer airs. They tell it like it is. Offensive linemen in the NFL are the closest that any other professional athlete comes to players in the National Hockey League.

People who have had the pleasure of covering more than one professional sport will almost always tell you that NHL players are the easiest to deal with. Like most NFL offensive linemen, NHL players on balance are polite, pleasant, honest, and endearing. Maybe it has to do with moving away from home at a young age to play junior hockey. Perhaps they understand that for most fans, they play the least popular of the major professional sports, and they've learned the hard lessons of humility.

But it's been my experience that among professional hockey players, there is a subset of even more self-effacing people. They have been known variously as fighters, tough guys, enforcers, role players, protectors, and even goons—but not by me. I hate that last term most of all; I find it demeaning and derogatory. It makes men like that seem somehow less than human.

My last fight was probably at the age of 12, against my younger brother Steve, and he may well have kicked my butt. I've never been punched in the nose, never had my jaw broken, never had an overhand right fracture my orbital bone, and never suffered a concussion because of being punched into submission. I've never done or suffered any of those things, but I've always been fascinated by people who have.

I've called more than 2,000 professional hockey games, and some of my best memories involve calling fights. It might have been Archie Henderson against Jeff Brubaker, it could have been Mel Hewitt against Dennis Polonich, perhaps it was P.J. Stock versus Stephen Peat, or maybe it was Byron Dafoe against Patrick Lalime (goalie fight!). It's been said that no one goes for a popcorn or a beer during a fight, and there is probably no play-by-play announcer who will tell you he or she didn't enjoy calling a fight.

I spent seven years riding the buses in the American Hockey League, and some of the best friends I have in the game came as a result of those 12-hour rides from Halifax, Nova Scotia, to Portland, Maine, and beyond. I was blessed beyond measure to have spent another 15 years calling games in the National Hockey League and more than 10 years beyond that serving as the host of Boston Bruins games on NESN. That's more than 30 years in professional hockey, and tough guys have always fascinated me.

The purpose of this book is to give them a chance to tell their story. Every hockey fan knows the names Bobby Orr, Wayne Gretzky, Mario Lemieux, Sidney Crosby, and Connor McDavid. Players like that are the best of the best, and they sell tickets and bring fans into NHL arenas. Diehards know, but fewer peripheral hockey fans have perhaps heard, the names Archie Henderson, Paul Stewart, Dave Brown, Chris Nilan, P.J. Stock, Jay Miller, and Terry O'Reilly. But hockey is better for all their efforts as well.

My sincere hope is that you end up feeling as warmly toward these men as I do. If one of these guys played for a team that opposed your favorite team, you likely have a certain opinion of that person. My goal is to at least make you see these guys in a different light and maybe even end up liking them a little bit.

But, in the interest of complete honesty, there is something that needs to be said here. I always enjoyed a good scrap and I always enjoyed calling one. But over the course of working on this project, and even going back several years in my career, I've also grown and expanded my knowledge base as we've become better educated about the effects of head trauma, concussions, and chronic traumatic encephalopathy (CTE).

When I started calling games, a player was said (often by me) to have "had his bell rung." He was given a whiff of smelling salts and a moment to collect his wits and often sent right back into the fray. Thankfully, the sport has grown (somewhat), and the knowledge base has certainly grown. We didn't know what we didn't know, but most of that has changed. Now, a player can be called off the ice by a concussion spotter, required to go to a quiet room, and evaluated for a possible concussion. It's hard to imagine too many activities that can cause a concussion or head trauma more than an old-fashioned, bare-knuckle fistfight.

I don't look at fighting the same way as I did back in the late '80s and many fans don't either. Some of that change likely has to do with my age and thinking about things differently than I did as a younger man. I would like to think some of that change has to do with empathizing with the men involved and being concerned about their health and well-being. I can also say, however, that no one in this book told me he wishes he played a different way or in a different time.

But the change in mentality I've developed over the years does nothing to diminish my admiration for the men who played the game that way and the atmosphere that fascinated many and was admired by a large number too. It is certainly a different game played today, and the speed and skill are exhilarating. Many think it is a better and more enjoyable game to watch by most standards.

There is nothing written down, but NHL tough guys admit to playing by a code. People who are not hockey fans probably don't believe any of that. A common thing among non-hockey fans is the belief that hockey fighting is fake and scripted, and barely a small step above a WrestleMania card.

I've always felt that enforcers are like modern-day samurai warriors or like the heroes of the Wild, Wild West who have always fascinated me. I had the pleasure of coauthoring a book with Shawn Thornton (and the *only* reason he is not a subject of this book is because we've already written an entire one together), and he tried to set down the specifics of "The Code." It may vary slightly from player to player, but the basics remain the same for all:

1. You always—ALWAYS—stand up for a teammate.
2. You never start a fight with someone smaller than you.
3. You try to never unfairly exploit an opponent who may be at a competitive or physical disadvantage.
4. You respect almost everyone who makes a living the same way you do.
5. You understand that if today is your day, tomorrow might be your opponent's day.

You probably noticed some qualifiers in that last paragraph.

1. The one thing that is universal and never changes is standing up for a teammate. Every guy I've interviewed spoke with pride about defending teammates and always say it was the part of the job that gave him the greatest satisfaction.
2. You try to never start a fight with a smaller opponent—unless that smaller opponent has a similar skill set to yours, and unless he does something to warrant being challenged.
3. Tough guys generally try to never take unfair advantage of an opponent—unless they think that opponent has earned it.
4. Tough guys usually, but not always, respect other tough guys. They know better than anyone how difficult the job is and the toll it takes. But dig deep enough, and most tough guys will admit there is at least one other tough guy, maybe more than one, who doesn't deserve that respect. They usually speak of that opponent with disdain—privately, if not publicly.
5. They may understand the notion of "win some/lose some," but they always went into a battle expecting to win and were generally upset when they didn't.

This book is not necessarily meant to glorify fighting in the sport, but it is meant to honor and respect some players who are wildly popular among a large segment of fans—and, in some cases, the *most* popular players in the history of their respective franchises. It is meant to relive some of the great stories and shine a light on some of the greatest storytellers to ever lace up the skates.

So, I set about telling stories with people who are loved by hockey fans but generally get far less attention than the highly paid, skillful stars. I wanted to tell stories about players that perhaps not every hockey fan knows. I wanted to give a voice to players with a great tale to tell but not always with the megaphone to tell it. I wanted to talk to a specific group of professional hockey players. I wanted to talk to the *Tough Guys*.

CHAPTER 1

TERRY O'REILLY

TERRY O'REILLY was apologetic.

"I'm sorry I'm late calling you back," he said. "I was out skating."

The man was 70 years old (now 71) and had had both hips replaced and a left knee reconstructed for both ligaments and cartilage, so it led to a logical question.

"Why?"

"Because I wanted to see if I still liked it," he replied, with a smile that was evident even over the phone.

"And do you?"

"Well, not today. But ask me again tomorrow."

The story is a good example of the pride and passion that marked Terence Joseph James O'Reilly, one of the most popular players to ever wear the Boston Bruins uniform and arguably one of the toughest. In fact, I would say that there was never a player and a team better matched than Terry and the Boston Bruins. There is a large contingent of people in Boston of Irish heritage and an even larger portion who admire toughness, guts, and determination. O'Reilly's name might have made him popular in Boston, but his game made him a legend.

Terry was selected by the Bruins with the 14th overall pick in the first round of the 1971 NHL Draft from the OHL's Oshawa Generals. Even he admitted he was surprised he was a first-round pick. But he also had other options.

St. Louis University was trying to convince O'Reilly to come to Missouri and play college hockey, dangling a full four-year scholarship as incentive. The Billikens were just beginning their hockey program and thought O'Reilly would be a solid building block. He was told the university dressing room would be right down the hall from the Blues in the St. Louis Arena, and it was sold as a first-class operation.

The university flew O'Reilly to St. Louis and gave him a tour. Coincidentally, the Blues were scheduled to host the Bruins while he was in town, and the school offered him a ticket to see his first National Hockey League game with the team that ultimately drafted him.

After the Bruins drafted O'Reilly, he wanted to talk with the Billikens' head coach, Bill Selman. Terry was always thinking, and he needed information. First, he wanted to know what would happen if he blew his knee out after that first season. Was the four-year scholarship guaranteed? Selman just said, "Oh, that won't happen." O'Reilly asked, "What if you build up such a program that I'm no longer the asset you thought I would be? What if you want to replace me with someone else?" Selman admitted that the school would likely prorate the scholarship under those circumstances.

O'Reilly simply told Selman, "My dad is a milkman, and I'm one of five boys in my family. I don't even have bus fare to get to St. Louis from Oshawa, let alone pay for the tuition costs if the scholarship gets pulled."

O'Reilly told Selman that unless the scholarship was 100 percent guaranteed, he simply couldn't consider it. But he was also talking to the Bruins, who were attempting to get him to sign a contract with them. He told the Bruins, "You know I just got back from St. Louis, and they are offering me a full, four-year guaranteed scholarship, which is worth about $25,000." Some of that was true, I guess.

The Bruins had just won the Stanley Cup in 1970, and O'Reilly correctly guessed he would begin his professional career in the minor leagues. He argued that he would be gambling his "full scholarship" for a minor league salary in the American Hockey League, and he said he couldn't accept. Suddenly the Bruins offered a $25,000 signing bonus (to match his "scholarship" offer), which in those days was serious money. The team told him that the $25,000 would pay for his continuing education at nearly any college he selected.

O'Reilly accepted the Bruins' offer and then spent his signing bonus on a 1971 Oldsmobile Cutlass Supreme, a ski boat, and a cottage on a lake. He did sheepishly admit he took an occasional college class from time to time, although he never did get his college degree. But his professional career was set to begin, all because St. Louis University would not guarantee his scholarship offer.

Tom Johnson was the Bruins' coach when O'Reilly joined the organization. Johnson was the coach when O'Reilly was recalled from the Boston Braves of the AHL for the final game of the NHL season. O'Reilly even scored his first NHL goal (and was a plus-3) in a 6–4 win over the Toronto Maple Leafs on April 2, 1972. It was O'Reilly's only NHL action of the year, as the team went on to defeat the New York Rangers, four games to two, to win the Stanley Cup. But O'Reilly also never played another game in the minor leagues.

Harry Sinden was the Bruins' general manager when O'Reilly joined the organization. In fact, O'Reilly joined the team before Sinden did, but Harry got an earful from Bobby Orr about the player wearing No. 24.

"When I joined the Bruins, Terry had played there the year before," Sinden said. "Bobby Orr told me coming in, 'Harry, you've got a player here and you will not believe the way he plays! You don't know this guy, but you're going to see one of the best players to help the team win that you could ever have.'"

Johnson was promoted to assistant general manager midway through the 1972–73 season and replaced as coach by Bep Guidolin. The Bruins lost in the quarterfinals in Guidolin's first season and then were defeated by the Flyers in the Stanley Cup Final in 1973–74, after leading the league with 113 points. Sinden decided to make a change behind the bench and O'Reilly was paired with the perfect coach for him, Don Cherry.

"It was wonderful, playing for Grapes," said O'Reilly. "He had an incredible skill of having his thumb right on the pulse of the team. He kept us humming right along. If we started getting too cocky, he reined us in, and if we started to play a little too uptight, he would do something silly in practice to make us laugh and suddenly have a good time again."

Cherry had seen O'Reilly, first in the minor leagues, and didn't really know what to expect.

"I was coaching the Rochester Americans, and I saw him for the first time when he was playing for the Boston Braves," Cherry recalled. "I said to myself, 'Holy smokes! This guy can hardly stand up!' Then I saw him for the second time a year later and he wasn't exactly a gazelle, but he could skate!

"When I started coaching the Bruins, I said, 'I'm just gonna let him be.' Everyone tried to change him, and I might have tried to change some guys myself, but not him. He did his own thing."

Cherry also instilled a Three Musketeers philosophy of all for one and one for all. The players learned quickly that they were to stick up for each other, and that was music to O'Reilly's ears. The Bruins evolved into one of the toughest teams in the National Hockey League, and O'Reilly always said that Cherry was instrumental in making that happen. And Sinden knew that O'Reilly was exactly the ingredient his team was missing.

"I could never tell you in one sentence what Terry meant to our organization, and I'm not even going to try, but he was critical in our team becoming the Big, Bad Bruins," Sinden said. "We didn't give ourselves that name—it may have been Philadelphia or Montreal that coined the phrase. We had some players who were pretty rugged, but I worried that we would become easily intimidated when those players started to leave. We lost a little bit of that for a couple of years until Terry came along, and Terry O'Reilly saved our ass! We would not have had the identity that our team developed without Terry O'Reilly.

"He would not allow the Boston Bruins to be intimidated, and if you played with Terry you had better be willing to play that way too."

O'Reilly was (and still is) a kind, gentle man—but no opposing player would ever believe that. He knew only one way to play, and that was as if every shift were the last he would ever have. Coaches have said O'Reilly always played like he thought he was going to be cut, something he doesn't dispute.

"Except for a few years in the middle of my career, when I was on one of the top lines, and one of the top scorers, I always thought I was on borrowed time," O'Reilly said. "I always felt like I had to fight to keep my job."

O'Reilly's coaches certainly never felt that way, and Cherry came to appreciate that he knew exactly what he was going to get from O'Reilly every single game and every single shift. O'Reilly was always going to bring that passion and emotion he was best known for.

"He had that Irish temper. I remember one time in Atlanta, a great big guy grabbed Terry," Cherry recalled. "He didn't really want to fight, but he just grabbed ahold of Terry, and kind of made him look bad. The next time we played in Boston, Terry just crushed this guy, and he was just laying there on the ice. So I told Terry, 'Don't worry, Terry. I think he's going to be okay.' And Terry just said, 'Oh, I don't care. I don't care if he dies.' I think he was kidding!"

Behind Sinden's management and Cherry's coaching, the Bruins were beginning to develop into a particular kind of team, and it was one that opposing teams did not look forward to playing against. According to O'Reilly, the turning point may have been a game in St. Louis.

"I was terribly sick all day long," O'Reilly recalled. "I think I lost about 10 pounds in just one day! Don came to my room before the bus was leaving for the game, and he took one look at me and just said, 'You're staying here!'

"I missed the game that night, and the Blues had a pretty tough guy named Bob Gassoff, and he was running around pretty good out there on his home ice. We didn't really have the lineup to stand up to him, and that one game triggered Grapes to strengthen that aspect of our game. So he talked Harry into calling up John Wensink. By the time our road trip moved onto Los Angeles, John was flying in from Rochester.

"We had a number of guys who could play a physical game, but perhaps never fight, like a Donnie Marcotte. Peter McNab didn't fight, but he was a big, strong presence at center ice. Brad Park, a Hall of Famer, was tough as nails. But the addition of a guy like John, to go along with Al Secord and others, certainly helped change the perception of our team."

The Bruins became that one for all and all for one team Cherry had always envisioned. If you picked on one member of the team, you better be ready to answer to all of them. One of the times O'Reilly was sticking up for a teammate led to possibly the hardest shot he ever suffered on the ice.

"Our goalie, Pete Peeters, had sort of poked Chris Nilan with his stick behind our net, kind of egging him on," O'Reilly said. "I was at the other end of the ice, and I turn around just in time to see what was going on, and I go racing back to our end of the ice. A linesman got there before me and got ahold of Nilan, but Chris reached down behind him and curled up his right hand from his knees. He came up like a jack-in-the-box, and I had come flying in, out of control, and looked over the linesman's head just in time for Nilan to spring up and [he] just laid me open with one well-placed sucker punch.

"Of course, in our building and with our team, our goalie was never going to be challenged without our team responding. In this case, it might have been Pete who provoked the incident, but it was up to us to protect our goalie under any circumstances."

It was that exact same philosophy that led to one of the most famous moments in team history. It was 1979, and the Bruins were playing the Rangers at Madison Square Garden when all hell broke loose.

"What happened at Madison Square Garden in 1979 was simply an impulse," O'Reilly said. "Remember, back then, the glass behind the benches was only about two feet high. This fan started swinging at Stan Jonathan, and Stan covered his head with his stick. The guy grabbed the stick out of Stan's hands and started swinging it back and forth over the glass. He could have clocked anyone within range. He was like a madman! So it was just an impulse to put my foot up on the dasher and dive over to stop him from doing that.

"It didn't take long for many of my teammates to join me, and that's probably why I was suspended the amount of games that I was. I had the 'C' on my sweater and I was the first one over, so let's just say the league was not pleased. That cost me eight games."

O'Reilly only knew one way to play, and he played that way every single game of his career. He sometimes jokes about his "skill set," and he sometimes sounds like Liam Neeson in the movie *Taken* when he describes those skills. But consider that in the 1977–78 season, O'Reilly had 29 goals and 90 points in 77 games, and he followed that up with 26 goals and 77 points the following season. He finished his Bruins career with 204 goals and 402 assists for 606 points in 891 regular season games. Oh, and 2,095 penalty minutes. And in 108 career playoff games, he had 25 goals and 42 assists for 67 points and 335 penalty minutes. He also finished with a career plus/minus of plus-222.

"I told you I wasn't a very skilled player? Don't believe everything I say," O'Reilly said with a laugh. "I had a certain set of skills. I could see the ice, I could make plays. My skating held me back from being a very effective player.

"You can't go back in time, but I wouldn't change what I did or how I played. I loved playing the game, and I think that's why I was able to play the way I did. I loved playing with reckless abandon...all or nothing."

O'Reilly freely admits that the way he played the game of hockey was born of love. He loved to play, and he knew that if he wanted to continue to play, he had to bring that energy, passion, and physical commitment to the arena every night. Phil Esposito gave O'Reilly the nickname Taz, short for Tasmanian Devil, for the way he recalled the cartoon character's frenetic energy. He seemed to never take a shift off, let alone a game. For O'Reilly, there really was only one way to play the game. That actually made things difficult at times, because, as a coach, he expected his players to approach the game the same way. Not many players in the history of the game could successfully do that.

"I loved the game, and I loved playing the game, but with my set of skills I had to play it hard," O'Reilly said. "I was certainly not going to be a finesse player. I had to take the body and finish checks, and a lot of people I played against were offended when I hit them as hard as I did or as often as I did. Many of them

wanted to fight me, and that became kind of a natural conse-
quence of how I played.

"I caught Dave Schultz with his head down one night at the
Spectrum in Philadelphia. It was a good shoulder check to
the chest, and he went up in the air and landed on his back. He
was out for a little while and the trainer had to come out to give
him "sniffers" and tell him who did it.

"Now, I was already in the penalty box because the referee
gave me two minutes for charging. Schultz gets up and comes
barreling over to the penalty box with his stick over his head! I
stood up and put my stick up in front of me to block his stick.
I didn't leave the penalty box, I didn't threaten him in any way,
I just held the stick up to block him. The linesman came over
and shoved Schultz into his penalty box, and the referee points
to the two of us, giving us 10 minutes each. It was one of several
instances when I didn't have much respect for officials and the
way they handed out justice."

While O'Reilly says he wouldn't change what he did or how
he played, there was one incident from his career he admits he
wasn't proud of. It involved referee Andy van Hellemond and
cost O'Reilly the longest suspension of his NHL career.

"We were playing the Quebec Nordiques in the playoffs. It
was Game 7, which we lost, 2–1," O'Reilly recalled. "I had been
speared by Dale Hunter, and then he turtled on me. I was out-
raged, and I really wanted to get this guy. Andy came in and
grabbed me. Now, I've been in a lot of battles, and the linesmen
generally circle around and have a signal so they can jump in and
grab both guys at the same time. If one player is loose, he could
keep swinging, and you don't want to give one guy an advantage

like that. Andy grabbed just me, and although Dale didn't get any punches in, I was alarmed that I was being restricted by one official while Hunter was not being held back at all. I swung my arm in a backhand motion to swat Andy away, and I hit him.

"After I left the ice, I had a chance to watch it back, and I was upset. I thought that was a pretty poor example to send to young players who might be watching us. Striking an official was certainly not the image I wanted to send out there. It was the heat of the battle, and it was done, and I had to pay the price.

"I had to go up to Montreal for the hearing. Andy was almost like one of my teammates at the hearing. He was saying, 'Well, it wasn't really a punch, it was more of a shove.' I think Brian O'Neill of the NHL was trying to get Andy to make it seem like he had been assaulted, but Andy didn't want any part of that. I was suspended for the first 10 games of the next season and given the maximum NHL fine."

O'Reilly had actually been under an indefinite suspension from the NHL because he refused to attend an NHL hearing scheduled a month before on May 7. O'Reilly felt like he had been prejudged for his actions, and he refused, initially, to take part. Given the measure of his punishment, he may have been correct.

Given the way O'Reilly played the game, it's probably not surprising that it's taken a physical toll on his body. But interestingly enough, he claims the worst he ever got hurt didn't come from a fight at all. It was a combination of friendly fire from a teammate followed by a puck battle against a respected opponent.

"I had received a stick in the mouth in the previous playoff series against Buffalo," O'Reilly said. "Mike Milbury and I were going behind the net for a puck and we came together, and I got my teammate Mike's stick right in the mouth. I ended up with 10 stitches in my upper lip holding things together. We eliminated the Sabres and we moved on to play the Islanders in the next round."

I've pointed out to O'Reilly that there may only be two players with a special skill set who were known for a particular style of play to have their numbers retired: himself, and Clark Gillies of the New York Islanders. Of course, the ever-humble O'Reilly wanted to separate himself from Gillies immediately.

"Clark was a more skilled player than I was. He was the captain of a team that won five Stanley Cups, and he was a huge part of that. I certainly didn't enjoy playing against him!"

But the two players had a legendary history against each other, including that playoff series in 1983.

"Clark and I were racing into the corner for a loose puck as I was trying to get a shoulder in front of him to get an edge, and both of our arms were helicoptering," O'Reilly recalled. "I lost my footing and went right down on my face. I hit my forehead on the ice and cut my eyebrow wide open. I had to go in to get stitched up, and the eye closed up pretty quickly. I came out and had a couple of quick scraps with Clark and opened things up again. Later in the game, Garry Howatt started a third fight trying to get me out of the game, and he was shooting for that same spot, so I had to get restitched yet again. I was a mess that entire series, getting stitched and restitched. I don't miss that part of the game at all!"

It was exactly that kind of fortitude and attitude that endeared O'Reilly to Bruins fans everywhere, his teammates, and management. Sinden always appreciated that innate toughness.

"Terry was as tough a guy as has ever worn the Bruins uniform," the former GM said. "I say that without hesitation. He was a hell-bent for election, wild-swinging kind of a fighter, taking the chance that he could land some of those shots. He never left anything on the ice when it was time to show physicality or courage. He was never tricky about anything—he just came right at you and did it!"

After O'Reilly's playing days were over, he surprised some people by stepping behind the bench and becoming the head coach of the Bruins. It may have even surprised O'Reilly that while he found it difficult, he also found it rewarding.

"After I finished playing, I tried coaching, and it was a tremendous period of growth for me," O'Reilly said. "To go from playing the game and looking after my own individual preparation, focus, and concentration to having to look after the whole squad was certainly different. Now I had to worry about everything—practice, the game, power play, penalty kill. It was like going to university for three years. It may have been even more difficult than that because it was a crash course."

That toughness that made Terry O'Reilly a legend to Bruins fans? It didn't stop when he became a coach in the National Hockey League. New Jersey Devils defenseman Jamie Huscroft saw it firsthand.

"My first year in New Jersey I was playing with guys like Jim Korn, Ken Daneyko, and Dave Maley," Huscroft recalled. "We're playing against the Bruins at the Meadowlands Arena, and the home team would go off the ice first, then the visiting team would go off second because the two teams were right next to each other.

"So Terry O'Reilly was just standing there in the hallway and letting us go by. Jim Korn was probably about 6'5", and I'm not sure who said something to who first, but I was walking in line right behind Korn. All I know is I heard Korn say, 'F—k you!' and he didn't even get the 'you' out and O'Reilly hit him so hard—one, two!—and down went Jimmy! I never said a word! I couldn't even look at Mr. O'Reilly after that! All I could think is, *'Holy s—t, is this guy tough!'* We didn't even look at Terry. We picked up Jimmy and just walked him into the dressing room. Nothing was said! No media! No discipline! No harm, no foul!"

But while O'Reilly often found the work of coaching rewarding, life at home was making everything more complicated. Terry's son, Evan, was born in August 1983 and almost immediately suffered health complications from a liver condition. Many times as O'Reilly was working behind the Bruins bench it was with an eye toward home and the health issues his son was facing.

"Evan was going through a period while I was coaching when he was vomiting, uncontrollably, and he would have to be taken to the hospital. It only seemed to happen to him when I was away," O'Reilly said. "I remember being up in Montreal, coaching a game, and I got the phone call. Evan had been driven into Floating Hospital. We got back to Boston around 2:30 AM and I drove over to the hospital and let my wife go home and relieve the babysitter who was watching our other son, Conor. The hospital had a chair that would fold out into a cot, and I rolled it right next to his bed and I spent the night right there, before going to practice the next morning. It didn't take long before I lost interest in coaching. I couldn't maintain the intensity or the focus that I had before."

The Bruins were playing the Whalers in Hartford on April 2, 1988, in the final regular season road game of the year. The team

TERRY O'REILLY   15

lost a lopsided game but had an eye toward the upcoming Stanley Cup playoffs. O'Reilly simply wanted to get home. He had gotten word that Evan was having problems and not doing well. When the team hurried onto the bus for the ride home, there was a Cadillac parked directly in front of the bus on the spiral ramp, blocking their exit from the building. The team waited an excruciating 45 minutes while building personnel attempted, in vain, to find the owner of the car.

Finally, O'Reilly told the building official what he was going to do. He took a tire iron and broke the small vent window so they could get into the car. The plan was to put the car into neutral and move it out of the way. O'Reilly gave the building official his name and phone number with the promise to the car's owner he would pay to have the window fixed immediately.

Unfortunately, the plan failed. The car had a locking shift lever, and O'Reilly couldn't get the car into neutral. Plan B involved 20 professional hockey players, who piled off the bus and skidded the car aside so the bus could escape the Hartford Civic Center.

As O'Reilly said, "By the time we got to Boston, there was a warrant out for my arrest!"

But more importantly, O'Reilly was able to get home for Evan. As one of the symptoms of his liver condition, Evan would develop a debilitating urge to scratch himself all the time. O'Reilly would climb into bed with his son and hold his hands. The five-year-old would wrap his tiny hands around his father's fingers and hold on until he could fall asleep. If he began to scratch again, O'Reilly would speak softly to him and Evan would gently wrap his hands back around his father's fingers and fall back asleep.

What O'Reilly didn't learn until a few days later was that he had been charged with third-degree criminal mischief and tampering with a motor vehicle. The car's owner claimed that he never planned to press charges, but that he felt he had to.

A few weeks later, the Bruins, who were playing the Buffalo Sabres in the playoffs, were chartering home from upstate New York. Weather was threatening to close in on Logan Airport in Boston, so the pilot came on the PA system to inform the team they may have to land in Hartford to wait for things to clear.

O'Reilly ran immediately to Sinden and pointed out there was still a warrant out for his arrest in Connecticut and that state troopers could theoretically come on the plane and take him off in handcuffs. Luckily, the weather cleared, and the flight continued on to Boston. O'Reilly's case was taken care of later before he ever had to set foot in the state of Connecticut again.

But the fate of Terry O'Reilly's coaching career had been set. He was already admitting to losing his desire to coach and, more importantly, his need to be there for Evan. Sinden reluctantly understood where this was headed.

"Terry was on his way to becoming a great coach in the National Hockey League, but then his son got sick," Sinden said. "He came to me and said, 'Harry, I can't continue like this. I have to leave the team to be there for Evan, and it isn't fair to you guys.'"

Evan held on until May 22, 2018, when he finally gave up his courageous battle.

In the summer of 2002, Sinden made a call to Terry at his home in Salisbury, Massachusetts.

"I was up here in Salisbury, working on the top floor of a five-story building and trying to put together what I called a crow's nest," O'Reilly said. "It was a 14-by-14-foot octagonal room that you access by a spiral staircase from the top floor of the building I was occupying. I'm up there putting sheets of plywood down over the two by fours with my compressor and my nail gun. My cell phone rings, and it was Harry on the phone.

"He said, 'Hey, Terry, can you come into the office? I want to talk to you about something.' I've got this project going, and I've got a construction crew working, with building supplies coming and going. I said, 'Harry, it's two hours for me to leave the construction site and drive into the city and then come back. I'm running a crew out here. Can't we just do this over the phone?'

"He said, 'Well, I wanted to talk to you about retiring your number.' I said, 'I'll be right in!'"

Bruins fans may not have been shocked at the news, but O'Reilly seemed to be.

"I was certainly surprised," he said. "I was part of a team, and Don Cherry was most responsible for how we melded together. We had such a fine balance of skill and toughness. We had incredible skill players like Greg Sheppard, Jean Ratelle, and Brad Park. And at that time Rick Middleton hadn't yet had his number retired, nor Gerry Cheevers. I was part of a team that had half a dozen guys who could have been honored."

On October 24, 2002, the No. 24 made its way into the rafters at TD Garden (then the FleetCenter). Ray Bourque told the crowd that it was "awesome" to have O'Reilly's number hanging right next to his, "protecting me again."

The ceremony was an acknowledgment by Sinden, Bruins ownership, and the fans of O'Reilly's importance to the franchise's history. It delighted his teammates, who never underestimated how important he was to them, each and every night. For O'Reilly, his game was never just another night at the office but something he felt every player had to take responsibility for.

"I thought everybody had the responsibility of protecting your teammates. But in the real world, not everyone can perform that role, so you leave it up to half a dozen guys who are big enough and strong enough to deal with that," O'Reilly said. "There were also players who didn't like that part of the game at all. Gord Kluzak was one of the biggest and strongest guys out there, a smart player, a skilled player, but he was sort of forced into that role and he hated it. But he did it when he had to do it. Cam hated doing it. Clark Gillies hated it. Fighting for your teammates is a responsibility that is thrown on you because of your physical abilities."

In a world of tough guys, Terry O'Reilly stands out. He was the ultimate teammate and ultimate Bruin.

CHAPTER 2

PAUL STEWART

P AUL STEWART was born in Jamaica Plain, Massachusetts, but grew up in Dorchester and was part of a famous athletic family in the greater Boston area. His grandfather, Bill Stewart, was a referee in the National Hockey League and an umpire in Major League Baseball. Bill Stewart also coached the Chicago Blackhawks, including to a Stanley Cup title in 1938. Paul's father, Bill Stewart Jr., officiated football, hockey, and baseball all over the Northeast. He also taught and coached at Boston English High School.

Paul Stewart was born into athletic royalty. But you could almost say the story of Paul Stewart's life was a never-ending series of interesting meetings...on and off the ice.

Stewart was serving as a 13-year-old caddy at The Country Club in Brookline and picks up the story when the caddy master said, "Hey Stewart, take this man's bag down to the Primrose. He's going to hit a few shots, and you shag for him."

"I said, 'No problem at all,'" Stewart recalled. "He was an older gentleman and he had a Sunday bag, just half a dozen clubs or so. He stood on the hill on the 14th and just hit a few shots down the fairway.

"He said, 'Son, would you mind carrying my bag? We'll play down the 14th hole and come back on 9 on the Primrose.' After he played the two holes, he asked me to take his bag to his car because he was going over to the Woodland Golf Club. He said he was a member at both clubs, and I complimented his game, and said he obviously was a very fine golfer.

"He turned to me before he left, and said, 'They tell me you're Bill Stewart's grandson. I know he passed away last year, and I'm sorry for your loss.' I told the gentleman that my grandfather had lived a full life, and I was curious how he knew him. He said, 'Oh, I knew your grandfather from the NHL.' I asked who he played for, and he acknowledged he never played but had been president of the Bruins back in 1931. He might not have been good enough to play in the National Hockey League, but he was a pretty fine athlete in his own right. The gentleman was Francis Ouimet, who won the U.S. Open golf title in 1913 and was inducted into the World Golf Hall of Fame in 1974."

Years later, and early in Stewart's officiating career in the NHL, he was standing in line at Los Angeles International Airport. He sensed there was someone standing behind him in the airport line that he recognized, and he turned to ask if he could tell the gentleman a story. Paul Stewart *loves* to tell stories.

Stewart informed the man that his father had taught and coached the gentleman when he was a student at Boston English High School. When asked if his father had spoken highly of the man's athletic accomplishments, Stewart said, "My dad told me you're a nice Jewish kid from Dorchester. Your dad was a barber.

You always came to class on time, you didn't mess around, and you were barely adequate in track."

The gentleman "laughed and laughed," Stewart recalled.

When prompted, Stewart went on to say that his father was in ailing health, having suffered congestive heart failure. The man asked Stewart to deliver a note to his father, which read, "Coach Stewart—It was always a pleasure. Leonard Nimoy. Mr. Spock."

Bill Stewart Jr. died a few weeks later.

Paul Stewart is very intelligent, but you get the sense he fears others will not know how smart he is given the way he made his living. He has a tendency to quote fine literature (almost *always* correctly) and he likes to dissuade people of their opinion that he is just a lunkhead hockey player. He most definitely is *not*!

Paul also has a heart of gold, and we'll have more on that later. But when he was an NHL official and I was a Cub Scout leader in Bellingham, Massachusetts, I was trying to help the scouts raise some much-needed funds. I had the idea to do an autograph signing at a local elementary school and asked several of my friends from the sports world to help me out. Former Bruin Terry O'Reilly was there, as was former Patriots linebacker Steve Nelson. Also there, front and center and a large part of the party, was Paul Stewart. I've never known him to say no to a worthwhile cause.

The big question in Stewart's early life was how a kid from Dorchester went to the prestigious Groton School and then played hockey at Penn.

"It was quite an adjustment for me going to the Groton School," Stewart recalled. "I was going to school with a bunch of kids I had only known when I was caddying in the summers

at Brookline and Hyannisport. So I saw my classmates sitting by
the pool at Brookline after a hard day at tennis, sipping lemonade
out of those yellow cups with the squirrel on it. Suddenly, it hit
me—'Jesus! I don't think I'm rich!' It was a big transition for
me going to Groton, learning how to walk with kings but stay
in touch with the common man."

After a PG year at Groton, it was time for Stewart to decide
on a college destination. He had always had his heart set on an
Ivy League education, and he still speaks like a totally different
player than what fans saw on the ice. Given his family pedigree,
he had multiple opportunities to play in the Boston area.

"I spent five years at Groton and I spent my summers caddying at Hyannisport, living in a tent," Steward said. "From the
age of 13 years on, I was kind of on my own, and the last thing
I wanted to do was surrender my independence. My home life
was less than ideal, and my mother was difficult. She had a fond-
ness for five o'clock, if you know what I mean. I just couldn't see
myself coming home after five years at Groton and summers on
the Cape and going to what I considered a commuter school. I had
played against all those kids who went to BC [Boston College],
from schools like Matignon and St. Sebastian's.

"It was 1971 or 1972 and the U.S. was still in the middle of
the Vietnam War. I went down to enlist in the Marine Corps
because I decided I would rather go in the Marines than go to
Boston College. But the fact was I really didn't want to go home.
I didn't want to go to BC or Northeastern because I didn't want
to be home with my mother. My brother went to BC for a year,
then he transferred to UNH. My sister left home when she was
18. Life at home was difficult. My dad was such a good guy and

he married my mother and had four children, but he was always headed out the door—refereeing and umpiring and coaching. That was probably his salvation. My mother just loved five o'clock too much.

"Penn fired Jim Salfi as head hockey coach and hired Bob Crocker after Boston University passed on him. My dad called Crocker and told him I could handle Penn academically after five years at Groton, and Crocker told him to come down for a visit.

"I went down to Penn, met with the AD and spent an hour with the admissions director. When I was finished, I got together with Crocker and he just said he hoped things went well, and he'll let me know. I hopped on a plane back to Boston, landed around 6:00, and my father met me at Logan. He said, 'Let's go to Durgin Park and celebrate!' I said, 'Celebrate what?' My father answered, 'They just called. You're a Quaker!'"

Stewart was a Quaker in name only. Bob Crocker rarely played Stewart and often even left him back at Penn when the team traveled.

"When the varsity [team] at Penn left the practice arena, I used my key and stayed behind and skated for another two hours! I would check the game roster for every game and go down the list—no, no, no, no. My heart was broken every single game, but I learned toughness from my father and my grandfather, and I never gave up."

Stewart's father was a teacher, a coach, and an official, and money was tight for an Ivy League education.

"My main work study job was the assistant rink manager, but my family needed the financial assistance, so I had two or three different jobs," Stewart said. "I painted all the numbers on

64,000 seats at Franklin Field with a stencil and a spray can. I drove the Zamboni and I sharpened skates. I helped the Flyers carry their bags from our rink, where they practiced, to the Spectrum.

"I watched Rick MacLeish, Barry Ashby—God rest his soul— and Bob Kelly. They became friends, but when I watched them, I thought, if these guys can play in the NHL then so can I. Kelly said to me one day, 'You don't play much here, do you? Do you want to get out?' He handed me a *Hockey News* and said, 'Pick the worst team in the worst league and go there asking for a tryout.'

"I knew a couple of guys playing for the Binghamton Dusters of the American Hockey League and they were getting thumped physically, spiritually, and on the scoreboard. My friends happened to be in Philly playing against the Firebirds, and when I visited them, I asked if they thought I could get a tryout with their team. They went right to their coach, Wayne Claremont, on my behalf. Claremont told me to come to Binghamton.

I took my last exam at Penn on Tuesday, and I was in Binghamton on Wednesday. Crocker had already told me I wasn't going to play at Penn because I had already fought a couple of guys who were hazing me. I put one guy in the hospital, and I broke the other guy's cheekbone. Crocker told me I wasn't going with the team to Princeton, and I had a key, so I went to the rink. I took my equipment out, went down to the Greyhound station, and 14 dollars later I was on my way to Binghamton.

"I checked into the hotel, then I went over to the rink. A guy named Gordie was there setting up the electronics and everything for the next night. We talked and he gave me a tour of the rink.

"I went to practice the next morning, and the GM told me I was playing the next night against Buffalo. My first shift I picked up an assist, then I got in a fight and got cut. I went in and got stitched up—23 stitches if you're counting—came out, and went after the same guy again. I became accepted on this team almost immediately and had the opportunity to work my way up."

Another common theme from Stewart's career is that there were always people who didn't like him. Look: he can be an acquired taste, and not everyone accepts him for who he is. He rubs some people the wrong way, and there were always people who had problems with him, both when he was a player and a referee in the NHL. He seems to have accepted that fact, if not to wear it as a badge of honor. You get the sense that Stewart and management almost never see eye to eye, and even though he was considered by many to be a pretty good referee, the NHL didn't seem sorry when his career was over.

"The owner in Binghamton liked me, but the GM tried to trade me five times," Stewart said. "He tried to trade me to Utica, to Johnstown. But eventually people got to know me, and they knew I was honest and tough. I never said no, and I never backed down. You've got to use those tools in your toolbox.

"I was told that if I thought I was going to make it as a playmaker, I better start fighting! So I did that, and I set a record in Binghamton that still stands—273 penalty minutes in 46 games my first season and 232 penalty minutes in 60 games my second year. And that didn't mean getting misconducts. You had to pay the fine for misconducts and I was only making $225 a week. I was living in the Skylark Motel for $100 a month. But I was on top of the world and happy!"

Stewart's efforts in Binghamton did not go unnoticed. A guy who played the game the way he did could almost always get a chance, and Paul did get other opportunities to move up the hockey ladder. There were not an unlimited number of players who were willing to take on the enforcer's role, and there were even fewer who were really good at it. Paul was more than willing, and he was relentless.

"I got a tryout with the New York Rangers, and I even got to play in a preseason game against the Flyers, of all teams," Stewart said. "John McCauley threw me out of the game after just 81 seconds. I grabbed this kid, and I just smoked him—knocked him flat. Then I tried to grab the back of his sweater to pull him up and give him another whack. But I guess I got the back of his hair, and there was a new penalty that year for gross misconduct and McCauley gave me the boot after 81 seconds. I always say if I had stayed in that game and played well, the Rangers wouldn't have been able to get rid of me because, other than Nick Fotiu, they needed some tough guys.

"The Flyers had five tough guys and the Bruins had six or seven—and the Bruins' guys were also scoring 20 goals! Stan Jonathan just got with the right coach [Don Cherry], and Terry O'Reilly started with Bep Guidolin down in the AHL. These guys got a lot of chances to play and to be coached. I didn't get those chances."

Stewart continued his quest to get to the next level and toiled at a number of minor league locations. One of those was with the Philadelphia Firebirds, and in the 1978–79 season, he had perhaps his most famous confrontation at any level of hockey. He was in Portland, Maine, to play the Maine Mariners. It was Stewart's opportunity to do what John Wensink of the Bruins had done just two years prior.

"What actually happened in that game was I challenged their bench," Stewart said. "And they had guys like Jim Cunningham, Glen Cochrane, Dave Hoyda, and Mike Busniuk—a bunch of guys who were pretty tough and they all played like they were the f—ing Flyers. I had challenged them at the end of the first period, and we went off the ice. I was coming back on the ice for the start of the second, by the Zamboni entrance at one end of the rink. My old man came down to the runway and said, 'Be careful! They're gonna get you!'

"I skated out about 20 feet past the net and they jumped me, and my Firebird team just stood there. I took a s—t kickin', but I never gave up. I stood there and took every punch right in the face, and I gave back what I could, especially against Cochrane, a big kid. The first fight, I smashed Cunningham, and that's when the others jumped in. I ended up as teammates with Jim, and he was a pretty nice kid. Ron Hogarth was the referee for that game, and after the third fight he had to give me a game misconduct. In fact, I ended up getting fined $850 from [AHL president] Jack Butterfield.

"I went to my team's dressing room, and I gathered up my stuff. After what had happened on the ice, and how my teammates refused to come to my aid, I wouldn't get on the bus with the team after the game. I met the team in the hallway as they were getting ready to get on the bus and I handed my equipment bag to the coach and asked where the next game was and just told him I would get there. I checked into the Holiday Inn across the street and just stayed in Portland that night."

Is it any wonder that the name of Stewart's autobiography was *Ya Wanna Go?* Years later, when Stewart was a referee and I was the PR guy/broadcaster for the Maine Mariners, we ran into each other at the Cumberland County Civic Center. I told him to wait right there and that I had something for him. I ran back to my office, where I had found a photo in the file. The picture was of Stewart *after* he challenged the Mariners bench, and I was sure he would want it. He was battered and bloodied but unbowed, defiant to the last moment. Stewart seemed genuinely moved by my giving him the photo, and I'm fairly sure he's kept it ever since. We've also been friends ever since.

I mentioned that Stewart is very intelligent, but he also has a *long* memory. After what happened that night in Portland, he wasn't mad at the Maine Mariners (whom he actually kind of admired). He was *really* mad at his Philadelphia Firebirds teammates.

"I actually belonged to Cincinnati at the time, and Floyd Smith, the general manager, just hated me," Stewart said. "I had 241 penalty minutes in 40 games, but he just wanted me gone, so he sent me to Cape Cod the next season and I played for John Cuniff for a while. Then Smith sent me to Philadelphia to play for the Firebirds. I was making one-way money, so I didn't care! The Firebirds were the farm team of the Colorado Rockies, and they were all gutless like they showed in Maine. The next year when I played *against* them, I purposely went out in the warm-ups without my gloves and stick. I just skated around and popped guys. I think I popped about six of them."

While Stewart toiled in the lower minor leagues (with one-way money!), his Cincinnati teammates paid attention, and they did not like the way they were being treated on the ice with Stewart down in Cape Cod.

"Barry Melrose went to Floyd Smith, and said, 'We're sick of getting the s—t kicked out of us,'" Stewart said. "'Everybody on the team took a vote and we want Stewart back!' So they brought me back to Cincinnati for the rest of the year."

Make no mistake about it—the Stingers may have brought Stewart back to avoid a team mutiny, but the coach and general manager still didn't want to play him. He practiced, and he worked, and he waited for an opportunity that seemed like it would never come.

"The Stingers went on a 10-day road trip, and you can tell how much the coach, Al Karlander, thought of me when they left me at home," Stewart said. "I worked the whole time they were gone—I skated every day and sparred in a gym there in Cincinnati. When the team returned from their 10-day road trip, I attended the first practice when they came back. I was called off the ice to go to the GM's office, and that's almost never good news, but I was told I had just been recalled by Quebec and I was playing in Boston the next night. I jumped right up in the air and pushed my hand through one of the ceiling tiles."

Stewart was about to make his National Hockey League debut, in Boston, against the team he grew up rooting for, the Bruins. He couldn't get out of Cincinnati fast enough.

"I flew into Boston that night and went to Mass General Hospital to see this little neighbor of mine, Christos Kaldis, who was dying of leukemia. I told him I was playing the next night against the Bruins, and I promised I would wave to him.

"I stayed at my parents' house that night and the next morning I went to Northeastern to skate with the Huskies, because the Nordiques didn't have a game-day skate scheduled in Boston. I told the Northeastern players I was going to put on a show that night they would long remember.

"The backstory is that the Bruins were incensed with Robbie Ftorek, stemming from the game they had played on Tuesday of that week. The reason the Nordiques were bringing me into Boston was to protect Ftorek from the Bruins.

"It was a Thanksgiving game, so everyone was off and I think I needed almost 50 tickets for all my friends and family. I was walking up the ramp of the old Garden, and I ran into Bobby Miller of the Bruins. Bobby's dad had a summer league in Billerica, and he used to let me play up there. I told Bobby, who was a friend of mine, 'I understand a few of your teammates want a piece of Ftorek, so I'll be right here in front of the Bruins' dressing room, and you tell those guys if they want a piece of Ftorek to come on out here and we'll do this right now. If you want Ftorek, you've got to go through me.'

"Cashman and O'Reilly came to the door of the dressing room, and Cashman says, 'You're f—ing crazy!' I answered, 'Here or out there, it don't matter to me. And you're first!'

We go out for warm-up. I'm going clockwise and Cashman is going counterclockwise, and he spears me. I chased him right into the Bruins' end of the ice, and we were both swinging our sticks."

That was only the "warm-up" for what would be one of the wildest nights in the history of the old Boston Garden. Stewart had promised the Northeastern players they wouldn't forget that night, and no one else would either. But no one tells a story like Stewart, so we'll let him recall in it in his own words:

"I seem to remember the Bruins were winning something like 2–1 or 3–1, and a lot of the guys on my team were a little bit nervous. Every time Ftorek went out on the ice, I went out. After a rush to the net, O'Reilly spears Wally Weir behind the knee, like a little invite. I stepped in front of Weir, and I said to O'Reilly, 'You fought *him* on Tuesday, but I'm the Thursday guy!' We dropped the gloves, but the linesmen jumped in. Dave Newell gave us two minutes each for delay of game.

"I'm sitting in the box, and Cheesy [Gerry Cheevers] was the spare goalie. O'Reilly and I are sitting in the box, and I told Cheesy to throw a bottle of water over. He told me to go f—k myself. I stood up and told him I knew where he lived in Lynnfield, and I was going up there after the game. The penalty box attendants were from Charlestown, and I told Cheesy he would need 10 guys from Charlestown to stop me.

"We stepped out of the box, and I'm standing on the red line when O'Reilly came right at me. I had watched those guys and I knew about O'Reilly and that big looping overhand left. He came and I dropped down and hit him with an uppercut. As the linesman broke us up, I asked if I was going to be able to fight him again. He just said, 'No, there's gonna be other guys coming.'

"Gary Doak skated by me in the box, and I really respected his game, but he told me I would be leaving the Garden in a hearse. I stood up and said, 'Hey, go back to the bench. I'm only doing heavyweights tonight.'

"Stan Jonathan skated over and just stood there. I told him to wait around because I would be out in three more minutes, and he was next. I go out for my next shift, and he comes running across at me. Right at the end of our fight I staggered him. I hit him with a right cross on the left temple. I had already watched his fight with Pierre Bouchard about 20 times, and I knew how he wanted to fight. He wanted to get in tight like he did with Bouchard, and I kept pushing him back.

"As we clinched, he said, 'I won. I cut you!' I told him 100 guys had cut me; that was nothing to brag about. I told him we could go again if he wanted, but Newell skated in and told Jonathan he was gone because he had a cast on his hand and he got a five-minute match penalty.

"I just assumed the next guy was going to be John Wensink because we had fought earlier in the AHL in New Haven, and he kind of stung me a little at the start of our fight. By this time in the game, we were losing something like 7–3 and there was only a couple of minutes left. They dropped the puck, and this guy's gloves were off and he is coming at me, but it wasn't Wensink—it was Al Secord. We both flipped to the ice, and he was trying to throw punches while we were down, and I stuck my finger right up his nose, and that ended that.

"I told him, 'Kid, I don't even know who you are, but if you want to make your bones with me, just stand up and we'll go out to the big B in the middle of the ice, and really give them their money's worth.'"

But Stewart was not going to get a chance to "go out to the Big B" for another bout. Referee Dave Newell had to break the news to Stewart after his fight with Secord.

"Newell told me that was my third fight and I had to go," Stewart said. "I had fun, I put on a show, and the only thing I didn't do was score a goal. I thanked Newell and headed for the gate when I remembered my friend Christos. I was at the runway next to the Bruins bench, and I stopped, turned around, and waved.

"Everybody thought I was hot-dogging it, but I was just keeping my promise. His sister, Mary, told me he was watching that night, and he got a big thrill when I turned and waved to him. Christos Kaldis died two weeks later, and they buried him in my Cape Cod Freedoms jersey. I still get emotional whenever I think of him."

Stewart's playing career effectively ended in the 1981–82 season after he played with the Cape Cod Buccaneers. He finished by appearing in two playoff games the following season with the Mohawk Valley Stars, and while his playing career was over, Stewart's days on ice were not yet done.

To the surprise of many, he went on to become an NHL referee. Paul officiated 1,010 regular season games, 49 Stanley Cup playoff games, the 1987 and 1991 Canada Cups, and two NHL All-Star games. He was every bit as colorful as an official as he was as a player, something that did not always sit well with his NHL bosses. In the modern NHL, the money is so high that players do not often need to seek a post-playing career. And even those that do almost never consider the possibility of serving as an on-ice official. The game would be well served if more former players wanted to do it.

I saw Stewart officiate a game in Binghamton early in his career. As was often the case in those days in minor league hockey, a fight broke out on the ice, and every player from both teams was involved. Each linesman was busy trying to separate combatants, and the usual job of the referee (only one in those days) was to stand off to the side and take notes on the penalties that need to be meted out.

But Stewart didn't even hesitate. He waded into a pretty good scrap and had opposing players in each outstretched arm, trying to calm things down. He looked at one of the players and yelled, "Do you want to fight with this guy?" He got a rousing "Hell, yes!" He looked at the other player, and asked, "So do you want to fight with this guy?" After being reassured that the player was in fact more than ready, Stewart simply stood back, let go of each player, and said, "Okay, go ahead!"

After his officiating career was finished, Stewart had an eclectic group of positions. He served as men's and women's director of officiating for the ECAC and even took a position as a judicial and discipline consultant for the Kontinental Hockey League in Russia.

Whatever you think of Paul Stewart as a player or an official, you should know his heart is as big as his ego. He has never hesitated to help when asked for any charitable endeavor and often met with young people after games. As far as what he hopes you think of him, when all is said and done, he puts it succinctly: "I hope the priest says about me, 'You can say whatever you want, but that guy never quit. He was tough, but he would help anybody.'"

Amen.

CHAPTER 3

ARCHIE HENDERSON

ARCHIE HENDERSON LOOKS and sounds like your kindly elderly grandfather…that is, if your grandfather were 6'6", weighed 220 pounds, and had fought bare-knuckle against hundreds of people over several leagues from junior to the minor leagues to the NHL. That is, if your grandfather were rumored to have sharpened a nail on one of his fingers to make it easier to gouge an opponent's face in a post-fight scrum. That is, if your grandfather had an opponent swing a hockey stick like a baseball bat across his face and get suspended for life for that infraction. But hear me out—Archie Henderson is one of the friendliest people I've ever met in the game of hockey. Then again, I never fought him.

Henderson was born in Calgary, Alberta, in 1957, the son of Frank (now 86 years old) and Doreen (now deceased). He had a brother, Don, built along similar lines, so you have to have some sympathy for Doreen and what her daily life was like raising those two.

Henderson had never been outside the Calgary city limits when he was given the opportunity to try out for the Lethbridge Broncos of the Western Canadian Hockey League. He had to talk his parents into allowing him to even take the tryout, because they were determined he was going to get his college education and make his way in the world.

"I never expected to be able to play Junior A hockey," Henderson said. "I was a very, very good student in high school and no one in my family had ever gone on to university. The one dream that my mother and father had was that I would be the one who would do that. They were blue-collar people with hardly any education, and they wanted their son to be the one to get a university degree.

"When I got the letter to try out for the Lethbridge Broncos, there was a real conversation between my parents and me about whether or not I should actually go. They didn't want me to go that far away from home, and they wanted me to go to school. I was actually enrolled at the University of Calgary and had already graduated from high school.

"I really wanted to try, and they agreed to let me, but they said if I did make the team I had to agree to take university courses, which I *did*, at the University of Lethbridge. And they said if it didn't work out, I had to come home and go to school, full time."

But know this about Henderson—the man is a natural-born storyteller, and it stands to reason he's got a story about that first trip away from home and his opportunity to play junior hockey.

"Look, this story is kind of bulls—t, and it's grown over the years," Henderson began. "But when I left Calgary, I *had* never been outside the city limits, and I went to Lethbridge, Alberta, to try out for the Lethbridge Broncos. When I arrived in Lethbridge, I was actually late, and I was told the registration was done for the day when I arrived at the arena where I was told to report. But the Zamboni driver was there, driving around on the ice, and I waited for him to come off. I said, 'Mr. Zamboni Driver, I'm here for the registration.' And I showed him my tryout letter. He told me they were all done, and they had left already, but they were staying at the Marquis Hotel downtown. He told me if I went down there, I should be able to find someone who could help me out.

"Here's where the story starts to become kind of bulls—t. I walked up to the front desk and told the lady I was there for the tryouts, and my name was Archie Henderson. She looked and told me I wasn't on the list, and they didn't have a room for me, so I just slept in my car that night.

"The next day, I go to training camp, introduce myself to a coach, and show him my letter. I get a number, get dressed, and go out on the ice. For the next three days all I did was fight! I had five or six fights in the first three days. On the third day, I was told, 'You're out!' and everybody's jaw kind of dropped. I had been cut after just three days of tryouts.

"But I show up the next day, and I'm watching the team skate around, and I go see the Zamboni driver again and ask if I could use his room out back. He said sure, so I go back there and put on my equipment and step onto the ice. The coach flies over and says, 'Hey, I thought I cut you yesterday!' I looked him in the eye and said, 'You did, Coach. But that was yesterday! This is a different day.' I went on to play over 700 professional games.

"The reason I started telling that story is I was a guy who always had to work for everything he ever had in the game. A common trait for people who have been in the game a long time is that they never, ever quit. I ran a hockey school in Calgary for 24 years and I would tell the kids that story at the end of the school, and it seemed to get built up bigger and bigger and bigger.

"But the message was simply to never quit. Not just in hockey, but in school and in life—never, ever quit. Look, Archie Henderson really didn't have a lot of talent, but he made the most out of what he had, and he was able to extend that career in hockey to a lifetime."

While Henderson's story has been a bit exaggerated over the years to serve as a lesson to younger players, the truth was he made the Broncos but rarely got to play on a team that featured future stars Bryan Trottier, Brian Sutter, and Ron Delorme. When he did play, Archie did the one thing he was better at than most—he fought.

"When I finally made the team, and played in junior, I had to do what I did in order to stick around," Henderson said. "I had to find a way to stay and that was fighting, which in those days, back in 1974, was acceptable. In fact, a lot of people in hockey were actually looking for that stuff. I really didn't get much of a chance to play, and then I was traded to Victoria.

"I was picked up by a rather notorious gentleman, but a guy who changed the course of my life, named Pat Ginnell. I got an opportunity to not only do what I did, which was fight, but also to play."

Playing in the Western Canadian Hockey League was like a scene out of *Mad Max Beyond Thunderdome*—two teams entered, and one team left. One team forfeited its playoff series against the Victoria Cougars (prior to Henderson's arrival) rather than face the physical torment the games would bring. There were stories of several players who left the game forever because they didn't want to take the beating the games involved. At the top of the intimidation list was the New Westminster Bruins.

"The New Westminster Bruins were bigger than many teams in the National Hockey League," Henderson recalled. "The penalty minutes were crazy, not just on that team but around the Western Hockey League. You didn't have just one player, but you had several on most teams who were playing that way. The league became known as the wild and wooly Western Canadian Hockey League."

When Archie says the New Westminster Bruins changed the sport, he isn't telling a tall tale. The Bruins were so bad they not only changed the game, they got themselves kicked *out* of that game. It all goes back to a game on March 22, 1979, between the Bruins and the Portland Winter Hawks at the Queens Park Arena in Vancouver—better known as The Zoo.

New Westminster head coach "Punch" McLean had already run afoul of WCHL rules on numerous occasions. He had been suspended for 25 games the year before for punching an official and he had been jailed for assaulting a 19-year-old female fan at the Portland Memorial Coliseum.

In the final seven seconds of that game in March, with the playoffs looming and Portland leading 4–1, there was a fight between Portland's Don Stewart and John Ogrodnick of the Bruins. On the faceoff after the fight, McLean sent two extra players onto the ice trying to goad referee Terry Gregson. Gregson, in frustration, awarded Portland a penalty shot and McLean attempted to insert his legendary tough guy Boris Fistric to play in goal. You heard that right—McLean wanted to put Fistric, a defenseman, in to play goal for the penalty shot. To put Fistric's game in perspective, he had 414 penalty minutes in 69 games in 1977–78, followed by 460 penalty minutes in 64 games the following season. In a 10-game stint in 1979–80 he amassed 99 penalty minutes in just 10 games.

With four seconds left in the game, McLean was determined to make a "statement," while Portland coach Ken Hodge was just as determined to avoid suspensions for any of his players before the upcoming playoffs. Hodge sent team captain Blake Wesley to try to convince referee Terry Gregson to call the game. The Winter Hawks knew what was coming, and the fans knew what was coming, but Gregson refused and dropped the puck.

McLean had sent all of his toughest players onto the ice for the final draw and the players' reaction to the start of play was immediate—an all-out brawl broke out all over the ice. And to make matters worse, McLean emptied his bench while Hodge refused to let his players go onto the ice, again fearing playoff suspensions. The Portland players on the ice paid the price.

Future NHL player Blake Wesley related what happened in a story from *The Oregonian* written by Paul Buker on March 5, 2000.

"Everybody squared off after the face-off, and immediately this guy named Boris Fistric skated over to me. He said something and I pulled him down. After that, it was like being on the cross and being crucified. Two guys came in, grabbed each arm, and they were sucker-punching me at will. After a period of time,

I couldn't see any more; my eyes were swollen shut. I tried to crawl to the bench.... I was told later a police officer helped drag me off the ice."

Wesley wasn't the only Portland player trying to escape the carnage. On several occasions other Winter Hawk players trying to leave the ice were grabbed by New Westminster players and dragged back out.

Wesley told Paul Buker, "Both my eyes were shut tight. I had a fractured orbit, a fractured cheekbone. I know if something like this had happened today, I'd be a very rich man. We had a six- or seven-day break, and I healed up and played in the playoffs, but there were a lot of emotional scars from it, too. You can't go away from something like that without feeling a tremendous amount of animosity to the organization and the players on the team who did that."

In that same story written by Buker, Portland play-by-play announcer Cliff Zauner described what he had seen on the bus after the game.

"When Wesley came on the bus, he was almost unrecognizable. His head was beaten to a pulp. They just disfigured him. If I didn't know him by his red hair and the fact he was supposed to be sitting in that seat, he would have been a stranger to me."

Even the New Westminster fans had seen enough. After the first few seconds, New Westminster fans began to boo. They were booing their own head coach, "Punch" McLean. Ultimately, eight Bruins players were suspended, and McLean was suspended indefinitely. The case ended up in a court of law, and seven New Westminster players were convicted of assault. McLean was out of coaching for good within two seasons. The local radio station that broadcast the New Westminster games refused to do so in the playoffs, citing listener complaints. The New Westminster Bruins ended up relocating to Kamloops in 1981.

Blake Wesley was drafted that summer by the Philadelphia Flyers in the second round, and he began his professional career that fall with the Maine Mariners, where I was also beginning my broadcasting career. He was well known for that flaming-red hair and a willingness to play physically. He went on to play 298 games in the National Hockey League, while his brother, Glen, was a first-round draft pick of the Boston Bruins and played in 1,457 games over a 20-year career.

That was the game of hockey that Archie Henderson grew up in during his junior hockey days. But as rough and tough as he was, even he wondered how his sport had devolved to that level.

"I've often wondered where some of these guys ended up in life after their WHL careers," Henderson said. "Some of these players were *extreme!* Through time there have been many rule changes, going back to those very days in the mid-70s to now, that have eliminated a lot of that stuff. Quite honestly, there were kids who quit hockey because they didn't want to play against some of those teams. I can remember going into New West-minster when I played for Victoria—and we were a very big and tough team—and those were games you didn't want to play. We would make a 20-day road trip, playing all the teams on the way out, play a double-header against Flin Flon, then play everybody coming back. You played against every tough guy in every town, and it never ended."

Henderson's efforts playing primarily for Pat Ginnell opened up another opportunity for him, and he was drafted by the

Washington Capitals in the 10th round of the 1977 draft. The man who never expected to play junior hockey was suddenly being given the opportunity to play at the professional level.

"When I went to that first conditioning camp for the Caps in Ottawa, that was where I met Tom McVie," Henderson said. "I'll never forget—when I went there they did all this testing. Tommy was really a bit ahead of his time. My body fat was through the roof! I was probably 25 pounds overweight. What the Caps didn't know was that I had had to have a summer job to make ends meet, and I worked in a bakery."

"Tom McVie wrote me a note, which I still have today, that said, 'This is the weight that you need to report at, and this is what you have to do as far as sit-ups, push-ups, and whatnot. And you have to run the mile in 5:40.' So I did everything that he asked—I lost all the weight and came in at 207 pounds, I ran the mile in exactly 5:40, I did the push-up numbers that they wanted and the sit-up numbers that they wanted. I didn't have a contract—I was a 10th-round pick! But Tom McVie and Max McNab wanted to start me on a pro career, [so they] signed me to an IHL contract and sent me to Port Huron."

Those who only saw Henderson play later in his career might not believe this, but he was a legitimate prospect as he began his career in the IHL.

"We had a pretty good team in the Port, with a number of Caps prospects, and I scored 16 goals," Henderson said. "That earned me a promotion to the American Hockey League for the Hershey Bears. Gary Rissling and myself set penalty minute records in Hershey [337 PIM], but I also scored 17 goals, and I was a real hockey player at the start of my career.

"I hit some bumps in my development and as time went on, I was cast in the role of veteran enforcer, who basically took care of the younger guys. And in the last part of my career, I took a lot of pride in that. I hoped that I might have helped, with a little bit of experience and some physical play, to develop those younger players as they moved on to the NHL. There were many, many, many players who came into *my* dressing room—or our dressing room—and went on to play in the National Hockey League."

Henderson was also involved in one of the most infamous incidents in hockey history—an incident that led to a lifetime ban from the sport, but not for Henderson.

"We were playing against the Grand Rapids Owls in our rink," Henderson said. "We were beating them, and we went to a face-off to the left of their goalie. I was playing right wing and was on the inside of the circle, and Gary Rissling was on my line, standing right in front of me at the hash mark.

"Gary was lined up against Rick Dorman, an IHL player who played many years of pro hockey. He was a real fighter from Manitoba and had a history of a lot of penalty minutes. Gary and Rick started jawing at the circle, [then] the puck gets dropped, and they're fighting. A couple of other guys jumped in—a guy named John Flesch kind of jumped onto Gary. So I grabbed Flesch and all hell broke loose! Everyone on the ice was fighting.

"I fight John Flesch and during the fight Flesch starts screaming, 'My shoulder! My shoulder! My shoulder!' I was kind of rag-dolling him around, so I thought I had injured his shoulder and I stopped fighting. Everyone gets broken up, except for Gary and Dorman, who just would not stop. While I'm starting to let Flesch go, Willie Trognitz comes in from the side and suckers me.

"After they break things up, I go looking for Willie. As the officials are breaking things up, Willie is over by the Grand Rapids Owls bench and Nick Polano, their coach, has his hand on Willie's shoulder. I come at Willie like I'm going to settle the score, because he had just suckered me. I skate up to him and assume a stance like I'm ready to fight. He didn't have gloves on, but he had a stick in his hands, and when I got close enough to him Trognitz swung that stick like a baseball bat and hit me right across the face.

"I went down on one knee, and the officials jumped in. I got up, but I had a broken nose and a concussion and had blood running down my face," Henderson said.

Trognitz earned a record 63 penalty minutes for this one incident.

"The next bit is kind of a blur, but the fans started coming down out of the stands and some of them tried to get into the Grand Rapids bench to start fighting with Polano and anyone else they could grab," Henderson continued. "One fan punched Trognitz in the temple before running off.

"When they finally did get me off the ice, our dressing room was actually upstairs above the Grand Rapids dressing room. I'm in the training room, and I'm really kind of out of it. I didn't even know if the game continued or if they stopped [it]. Morris Snyder, our GM at the time, came into the dressing room to check on me. I didn't even know where I was. They took me to the hospital, and I had to stay overnight for observation.

"Bill Beagan, the IHL commissioner, decided he had seen enough and he suspended Willie Trognitz for life. Rightfully so, because what he did was ridiculous. I didn't have anything to do with any of that. I was a young player trying to make my way, and I didn't really want to be involved."

Four days later, the Cincinnati Stingers of the World Hockey Association signed Trognitz to a 10-game tryout. Stingers coach Jacques Demers wanted protection for some of his smaller players, especially the highly skilled Robbie Ftorek. Trognitz's "lifetime" suspension cost him four days away from professional hockey.

Trognitz was paid $150 per game over the course of his 10-game tryout with Cincinnati. He dressed in all 10 games and played in seven. He had 37 penalty minutes, but 25 of those came in one game against the Quebec Nordiques. He was offered another 10-game contract, but he declined, saying, "What's $150? I've got guys making $150,000 hiding behind my back."

But if you think that's the end of the Archie Henderson–Willie Trognitz story, Henderson shared the kicker.

"A couple of years later, I'm in Hershey, Pennsylvania, and Gary Green, the youngest coach in the history of the NHL, became the head coach of the Hershey Bears. For whatever reason, Gary Green didn't like Archie Henderson. He didn't dress me or play me, and it came to a head. Green actually said to me in a meeting, 'You know, Archie, have you ever thought about going into real estate?'

"It was a sad part of my career, but I was forced by Green to leave the Hershey Bears. We loved Hershey, and it meant a lot to me to play for the Hershey Bears. My old coach, Ron Ullyot, had gone to the Fort Worth Texans of the Central Hockey League. Ron called the Caps and asked if I was available, and it was agreed I would be loaned to the Texans.

"Alice and I packed up our stuff and started to drive to Fort Worth. This was long before cell phones. I was about halfway there, and I had to call Ron Ullyot from time to time to let him know where I was and when I expected to get there. The Texans were in last place, and Ron was anxious to get me there for a certain upcoming game.

"I said to him, 'By the way, Ronnie, can I wear No. 19?' That was the number I wore in Port Huron and the number I wore in Hershey. The phone kind of went silent, and he said, 'Well, we've already given out No. 19.' I just told him to take it back and give it to me because that was *my* number.

"I asked him who had No. 19, and he kind of quietly said, 'Willie Trognitz.' I was driving from Hershey to Fort Worth, and I had no idea he was even on the team. He had just been signed by the Texans on a tryout agreement.

"Now I'm in a bit of a dilemma. Do I really want to do this? Do I really want to go to Fort Worth? I get there and the first day I walked into the dressing room, the room went totally silent. My stall was directly across from Trognitz's. The first couple of days we didn't even speak.

"Then we were getting on the bus to go to Dallas for my first game. I usually sat near the front of the bus, a couple of rows behind the coach. I heard guys kind of murmuring and laughing, and I could hear my name. I stood up and walked back, and there's Willie telling his story about what happened, but his version wasn't exactly the way I remembered the whole thing happening. So I confronted him right there on the bus. I told him that if he ever spoke out of line, or didn't tell exactly what had happened, that I would kick the s—t out of him!

"I went back to the front of the bus, and we never had another problem. And—are you ready for this? We played on the same line! That team went from dead last to the seventh game of the finals of the CHL, losing to Salt Lake.

"Now, I haven't spoken to Willie Trognitz since that season ended, but we were teammates and we did play on the same line. I wouldn't say we ever became close, but we did have a lot to do with helping that team go as far as they did.

"I never really looked for him again, but I heard he became a tugboat operator in Thunder Bay, and he saved some people's lives in a storm and received some high honor. For that I tip my hat, *but* I will never forget what happened. It was really bad, and there was no need for it.

"Do I regret not confronting Willie more than I did? No...I don't. In those days, that's the way it was. Was it a cheap shot? 100 percent! I would never want my son or Willie's son to ever be involved in something like that. I've always tried to be honorable when it came to things like the fighting part of the game. But that was just a bad situation."

In a *Sports Illustrated* story by the illustrious Peter Gammons, Trognitz gave his side of the story.

> There's no question that what I did was wrong. I hit him on the head with my stick, and stick swinging can't be part of the game. But I'd already finished a game, I had had two fights, and I was exhausted. This giant lunatic charges me, screaming, 'I'm gonna kill you,' so I reacted, figuring he'll never eat five feet of lumber to get at me. They told us before the game that Henderson was a bloody lunatic, and I was just trying to get him to stop.

Henderson continued his career as something of a Western gunslinger. He was always the marked man, and he always had players looking for him. He fought almost every night, but he always, as he says, tried to fight with honor. Consider the numbers—in his professional career, Henderson played in 775 games, regular season and playoffs, and accumulated 3,287 penalty minutes. His NHL career lasted only 23 games with 92 penalty minutes. That followed his four-year junior career of 187 total games with 786 penalty minutes.

"I remember fighting with Jeff Brubaker three times one night in Halifax, Nova Scotia," Henderson said. "We fought the first time, and when the penalty was up, we left our sticks and gloves right in the penalty box and went a second time. Later, we fought for the third time and earned the game misconduct. I kind of rocked him in that last fight, and I could see he was kind of out of it, so I didn't throw a last punch. I just let him down to the ice. Jeff would have done the same thing for me. He was always a respectful kind of fighter."

I was the voice of the Maine Mariners at that time and called that game and all three of those fights. In that third and final fight, right at the center circle, Henderson had his right hand cocked and ready to throw when he realized that Brubaker was probably out on his feet. I watched him hold back on the punch and calmly lay Brubaker down on the ice. Respect was a real thing for hockey tough guys.

When I began my career with the Mariners, they were the minor league franchise for the Philadelphia Flyers. The Mariners played the game and were built the same as their parent franchise. That meant the Mariners were big and tough and more than willing to fight. I had been around hockey tough guys since the beginning of my career, with pugilists like Glen Cochrane, Jim Cunningham, John Paddock, Jim Cunningham, Mel Hewitt, Daryl Stanley, and Dave Brown. But when Archie arrived, it felt slightly different. His exploits, especially at the minor league level, were legendary. But he always treated everyone with kindness and respect and was truly a gentle giant.

But imagine playing a game in which, night in and night out, you know the opposing coach has someone already selected to try and take on the king. For Henderson, that was almost always the case.

"I would go into Rochester, and I was always a bad guy going into that town," Henderson said. "I was kind of like a wrestling heel. I beat up some of the guys on their team, and their fans didn't like me. So the Rochester Americans under Mike Keenan brought in a guy named Val James. I think it was Val's first or second game in the American Hockey League. At that point no one knew who Val James was.

"We fight in the game, and Val was a very, very tough guy. In those days at the arena in Rochester both players went into the same door in the penalty box, and there wasn't even any separation in the box. There was just this little man, who was about 5'6" or 5'7", and an older fella, who had been the penalty box keeper for many, many years at that point. His job was to stand between the two opposing players.

"I think I was probably Val's first fight in the AHL, and we go into the penalty box, and this little guy is standing in between us. I'm sure Val was thinking, 'What is this little guy gonna do?' So I reach over and pat Val on the ass and say, 'Welcome to the

American Hockey League!' But in the AHL, I think Val was one of the all-time tough guys."

As is the case for every tough guy who ever played, it eventually becomes time to pass the baton. Inevitably there is a bigger, younger, stronger, and more eager player ready to assume the mantle.

"There was a belt, and for a while I had that belt, so that made me a bit of a mark," Henderson said. "If you could go after me, that would allow you to make a notch on your own belt. That happened with a guy named Bob Probert. The Mariners went into Adirondack and Probert was on that team along with Joey Kocur. By that time, I was over 30 years old, which is a bit older in my line of work. Bob was coming out of junior hockey, and he was trying to make his mark. So we ended up fighting in Glens Falls on a Wednesday and when we played again on Friday back in Portland, we squared off again in the neutral zone. But it was obvious Bob Probert was that next generation."

Henderson decided it was time to hang up the skates and the boxing gloves. He and Alice moved back to Calgary, and Archie was ready to go into private business. They wanted their kids to get settled into school and assume a more normal—less nomadic—life. Those plans lasted until Henderson received a call from the Chicago Blackhawks.

"They wanted to know if I would go to Saginaw, Michigan, and help out at the International Hockey League level," Henderson said. "They wanted me to play for the Saginaw Hawks. The team had a lot of young players, and they were in last place. I was kind of on the fence, and they asked if I could play defense. I told them that I had been a right wing my whole career, but that Tom McVie had put me back on defense a couple of times over the last couple of years.

"The head coach of that team was Dennis Desrochiers, and we had a history going back to my first year in Port Huron. He played for the Saginaw Gears and was a legendary IHL scorer and kind of a tough guy as well. We had a history of being combatants. Dennis reached out to me as well, and I agreed I would go there to play.

"But when I spoke to Bob Pulford and Jack Davidson it was with the understanding that if I did come out of retirement, I wanted to get into coaching as well. So I went to Saginaw and we had guys like Eddie Belfour, Bruce Cassidy, Warren Reichel, Dave Mackey, and others on the team. When I got there, we were in last place but we ended up going to the conference finals and lost to Flint."

That playoff loss to Flint was in a four-game sweep. Henderson knew that would be his last game, but he had to go out on his terms, and that meant one final battle with former teammate Jamie Huscroft.

"We had a really tough team in Flint with like seven tough guys, so Saginaw wasn't going to intimidate us physically, and we ended up sweeping them in the first round," Huscroft recalled. "We're playing Game 4 in Saginaw to complete the series, and we're up something like five goals with five minutes left in the game. Big Arch always stood on the bench, and he's standing there yelling at me, *I'm coming after you! You better keep your head up, Husky!* So I answered, 'Just f—k off, Arch! We're about to sweep you guys. Just sit down and shut up!'

"He jumps off the bench and I'm thinking, 'Are you kidding me?!' We fight, and we go down, and he's yelling at me, '*Husky!*

Keep your fingers out of my face!' And I just said, 'Archie—I'm not getting my fingers anywhere near that face of yours! I can only guess where that mouth has been!' I'm thinking, if he bit me, he would probably give me rabies!

"I had played with Archie for a while, and he always told me, 'There's two fights. One when you're standing and one when you both go down!' And he was not above trying to gouge you or pick your cheek with that nail—anything to win. And when the fight was over, he would always bark at the opponent, *'How'd I do? I did pretty good out there, huh?!'"*

Most hockey tough guys will tell you there is always something they regret—a particular play or a fellow combatant they would change if they could. Henderson has several.

"The one that stands out in my pro career was the night in Portland, Maine, with Robin Bartell," Henderson said. "Robin played for the Moncton Flames. I got hit by Robin behind the net earlier in the game, and he ran me a little bit and hit me really hard. In those days, you just didn't do that to me. I was one of those guys that you just didn't do that to. You let me sleep, or you just let me play.

"I told him at the time that it was a bad move on his part and he was going to get it before the game was over. We had scored a goal, and for some reason I was on the ice with about 10 seconds left in the game. Well, at the face-off circle the defenseman right in front of me was Robin Bartell.

"Tommy [McVie] was our coach, and I don't think Tommy realized what was going through my mind. I shouldn't have been on the ice. The puck was dropped, and it went back to Robin, and I left the right wing spot off the face-off, went directly at him, and cross-checked him right in the face. Down he went, and it was really bad—all hell broke loose. If I remember correctly, their bench emptied out and everyone was fighting on the ice. They got Robin off the ice on a stretcher, and I ended up getting suspended for 12 games.

"That's the one that has always stuck with me over the years—and there are several others that I could talk about, but I won't—that I would like to take back. But overall in my career there aren't a lot of regrets. I did what I had to do to stay in the game as a player. I wish I had been able to score 50 goals, but that wasn't in my skill set."

Talk to Archie Henderson today—I highly recommend that to anyone who has the chance—and you'll get a motivational speech. He'll compliment you on *your* career accomplishments and cover his own with self-deprecation. But make no mistake—when he was active, few players were more intimidating than Henderson, and few were more willing to do *anything* for his team and teammates. In a sport with no shortage of tough guys, Archie Henderson was one of the toughest.

CHAPTER 4

MILAN LUCIC

I F YOU ASK FORMER BRUINS tough guy and coach Terry O'Reilly who his favorite NHL player is, he doesn't even hesitate. It should come as no surprise that he immediately names another former Bruin, Milan Lucic. It did, however, surprise Lucic, who admits he didn't even know who O'Reilly was—at first.

"It's pretty cool! I didn't even really know who Terry O'Reilly was, other than in *Happy Gilmore* when Adam Sandler says his favorite player is the Tasmanian Devil," Lucic said. "Obviously, when I arrived in Boston, I learned a lot more about him. Now that I know him, and what type of player he was, that he was the captain, and what he meant to the city of Boston and his teammates, it's even more cool. And I also think it's kind of ironic that he and I have the same birthday! It means a lot that a guy like Terry O'Reilly would say something like that."

Milan Lucic stands 6'3" and, as Shawn Thornton once told me, "He walks around at 240 pounds on a comfortable day." To put that in historical perspective, on October 1, 1975, for the "Thrilla in Manila," Muhammad Ali was 6′3″, 224½ pounds. That's the kind of "heavyweight" power opposing players have faced when tasked with taking on the man his friends call "Looch."

Lucic says what physical advantages he may have come naturally.

"I was always one of the bigger guys both in class and in my junior hockey days," Lucic said. "I was usually the biggest guy on my team growing up. For whatever reason, guys look at me and think I'm 215 or 220 pounds, then I step on the scale and I'm 235. I was always just heavy and big-boned. My dad was also six feet and weighed about 220 pounds. The thickness that we had was a family trait—even my grandpa on my mom's side was also about 5′11″ and 205 or 210 pounds. So I guess I come by it naturally, and we're just a thick, heavier family."

Lucic comes from a proud Serbian heritage. In fact, both of his parents emigrated to Canada from Serbia.

"My dad came from Serbia in 1984 and my mom had come to Canada in 1969 when she was just two years old, with her parents. I was raised in a Serbian family. I didn't start speaking English until I began going to kindergarten. Even up until I moved away from home, I spoke Serbian in our home with my parents and my grandparents. Even now when I speak to my grandparents, I speak Serbian. Our family was always very in touch with our roots."

Lucic's grandfather on his mother's side is also the father of another NHL veteran—Milan's uncle Dan Kesa, who served as a role model for his younger nephews.

"My mom's brother, Dan Kesa, played in the National Hockey League with Vancouver, Pittsburgh, Tampa Bay, and Dallas. My older brother and I were kind of obsessed with my uncle because we had a member of our family playing pro hockey. We were so excited every summer when he came home. We spent a lot of time with his family. If you actually go look at his stats, especially in the Western Hockey League, he put up one of the best power forward seasons ever [62 games, 46 goals, 51 assists, 97 points, 201 PIM] for Prince Albert."

Kesa may have had one of the great power forward seasons in WHL history, but that was only until his nephew came along years later, playing for the Vancouver Giants. Lucic had those obvious physical attributes, but he readily acknowledges that there was one thing that set him apart from many of the other players in junior hockey.

"A big part of why I got noticed was my ability to fight," Lucic said. "I always felt that I was a good player at every level that I played—minor hockey, Junior B, Junior A, the WHL, all the way up to the NHL—and I felt I had the ability to score and play. But the reason why I was picked by teams at a younger age, and why I got extra chances and extra looks, was because I fought. That was one of the things my uncle told me—'You've got nothing to lose. You've got to do something to stick around.' And my parents were never opposed to me fighting either. If dropping the gloves helped me get noticed, then all the better. If it wasn't for my ability to fight, I'm not sure I ever would have gotten a look past Junior B. I was okay with that too.

"I played every sport that I could growing up. There was no football where I lived, but I played rugby and I even joined boxing when I was 15 years old. I boxed for two or three years, and was competitive at that, until I made the WHL. I loved hitting the pads and hitting the heavy bag and stuff like that. I'm the middle child with two brothers, all pretty close in age, so I guess I grew up having those "brotherly love" battles. It was always something that was in me. I never had an issue with fighting, and I still don't have an issue with fighting. Even when I was younger, it was something that I even looked forward to."

In Lucic's first season with the Giants, he had a rather paltry nine goals and 10 assists for 19 points in 62 games. But, he said, what kept him around for more than just a look was his 149 penalty minutes. It all came together for him in his second season with the Giants, when he exploded for 30 goals and 38 assists for 68 points, plus another 147 penalty minutes. But even better was his play in the ensuing playoffs.

The Giants had lost in the WHL finals to the Medicine Hat Tigers but were allotted a berth in the Memorial Cup tournament because they were the host team. The Giants went on to capture the Memorial Cup title by beating that same Medicine Hat team 3–1 in the deciding game. Milan assisted on the game-winning goal by Michael Repik, tied Repik for most tournament points with 19 in 22 games, and was named the winner of the Stanford Smythe Memorial Trophy as tournament MVP.

In February 2011, Lucic was added to the Vancouver Giants' Ring of Honor and was voted by the fans as the all-time best player in franchise history.

Despite all his junior hockey success, Lucic wasn't sure he was going to stick with the Boston Bruins when he attempted to make the team as a 19-year-old rookie in his first NHL training camp. Junior players are allowed to play up to nine games with their NHL team and still return to play junior hockey. If they play past the nine-game mark, they are required to stay at the NHL level. Any doubts Lucic may have had seemed to be answered on October 12, 2007, when the Bruins were playing the host Los Angeles Kings. Lucic had what is known in hockey as the Gordie Howe hat trick—a goal, an assist, and a fight.

"It started with a fight against Raitis Ivanans. Then I picked up an assist in the second period [on a goal from Aaron Ward], and I scored my first NHL goal in the third period [assists to David Krejci and Zdeno Chara] to cap it all off," Lucic said.

"The general manager for my junior team in Vancouver, Scott Bonners, was hoping the Bruins would return me to the Giants. I was going to be the captain and we were going for a Memorial Cup repeat. He said the minute I completed that Gordie Howe hat trick he knew I was never coming back. He jokes that I screwed him out of another Memorial Cup championship. That game and that night, and how everything occurred, probably allowed me to stay in the NHL that season. That was easily the most memorable game of my rookie season."

Lucic arrived at that first training camp on an incredible hockey high. And his perfect offseason continued.

"I was kind of on Cloud 9. We had just come off of winning the Memorial Cup, and I was the MVP of that team. Then we did a U-20 Canada versus Russia tournament for the 35th anniversary of the Summit Series, and things went well for me there too. I was playing a lot and I was feeling good about myself and my game. But it *was* intimidating coming to that first Bruins training camp.

"I remember my first game was in Dallas and you look across the ice and there's a guy like Mike Modano, not to mention that in your own dressing room, Zdeno Chara comes up to you and says hello. He's this mammoth of a man and mammoth of a hockey player. I had never seen a person or a hockey player that big before. But my mentality was just do my own thing, go out there and leave everything on the ice, and see what happens."

Lucic got past the nine-game tryout period to remain at the NHL level. He was told to move out of his downtown Boston hotel and find a place to live. He had made the Bruins as a 19-year-old rookie, but he also acknowledges that he was helped along the way by a number of Bruins veterans.

"Those physical veterans on that Bruins team—Shawn Thornton, Zdeno Chara, Andrew Ference, Shane Hnidy—helped me *so* much my rookie season," Lucic said. "To be honest, Shawn was trying to establish himself as an everyday NHLer as well that season. He and Z gave us two legitimate heavyweights above me on the physical pecking order. That took a lot of pressure off of me, and their guidance also gave me a lot of confidence. I had more conversations about that stuff with Shawn because we were playing on the same line, but other guys helped me too. I bet there were multiple games when Shawn and I fought in the same game.

"There may have been players who didn't want to play against the line Shawn and I played on, but honestly, there were players who didn't want to play against our *team* for a number of years there in Boston."

Hockey has always maintained that unofficial mentorship program. Shawn Thornton was shown how to comport himself as an NHL enforcer when his career began, and he passed that information on to the young man in his charge.

As a duo, those two were something to behold. Several years later, the Bruins' promotions department borrowed a theme from a popular movie franchise to pay homage to them. *The Blues Brothers*, starring John Belushi and Dan Aykroyd, came out in 1980. The sequel, *Blues Brothers 2000*, came out in 1998. In 2013, Shawn Thornton and Milan Lucic became The Bruise Brothers, spawning a poster that still hangs in Lucic's house to this day.

Lucic's third season with the Bruins came to an end with a gut-punch loss in the playoffs to the Philadelphia Flyers. The Bruins had a three-games-to-none lead in the series and then had a 3–0 lead in the decisive Game 7, with Lucic scoring two of those goals, before losing 4–3. That was just one of the things that drove Lucic during the offseason.

"It wasn't just that playoff loss," Lucic said. "I got injured twice…and I missed 32 games. It really wasn't a very good season for me. Then, personally, I had a pretty good playoffs, but we lost that series to the Flyers. So I had a lot of motivation to sustain me in the offseason.

"But I also don't know if we go as far as a Stanley Cup championship in 2010–11 if we didn't go through that loss to the Flyers. The loss motivated me more than anything, but I was doing whatever I needed to do to improve my game and continue my development. I used my good personal performance in the playoffs, but that gut-wrenching loss, to keep me going in the summer."

NHL tough guys will almost always step outside the lines from time to time and receive supplemental discipline from the league. Lucic's first incident came in the 2009 playoffs, when the Bruins were playing the Montreal Canadiens.

Lucic was given a penalty for cross-checking Canadiens forward Maxim Lapierre in the head, and the league held a disciplinary hearing. The Bruins, defending their player, argued that Milan had *not* cross-checked Lapierre, but the league disagreed and gave Lucic a one-game suspension.

"I didn't really cross-check him," Lucic said. "I know there was one replay angle where it looked like I did, but I know in my heart that I didn't. I have nothing to lose by telling a different story here, but if I really *had* cross-checked him in the head, he wouldn't have gotten up, I'll tell you that much."

Lucic's next big disciplinary issue came during the 2011 Stanley Cup championship season. The Bruins were playing the Atlanta Thrashers on December 23, 2010, when Freddie Meyer hit Lucic high and hard. The hit was egregious enough that Bruins defenseman Andrew Ference stepped in and began fighting Meyer. While that was going on, Lucic came over and punched Meyer as well. Lucic received a match penalty and was fined $2,500 by the NHL. The league then tagged on another $1,000 fine for Milan's middle-finger salute to the Thrashers bench. Oh, and he says he deserved it all.

"If it was today's game, I would have gotten more than just a fine," Lucic said. "And he deserved it, by the way. He hit me high, and that's why Andy responded. We had a line brawl, but that's what championship teams are made of...guys sticking up for each other."

That might have been the only blemish on Milan's 2010–11 season. His game blossomed with 30 goals and 32 assists for 62 points in 79 games. He had 121 penalty minutes. He tied his linemate, David Krejci, with those 30 goals, and spent much of the season playing on that line with Krejci and Nathan Horton. Krejci had to feel "10 feet tall and bulletproof" that season. In the Stanley Cup playoffs, Lucic added five goals and seven assists for 12 points and helped the Bruins win their first Stanley Cup championship in 39 seasons.

"It really was a perfect season for me," Lucic said. "Everything just went right. I still think about it all the time. That season was the best, most fun season I've ever been fortunate enough to be a part of. It was everything. My own personal season was great, but more important was the team success. Our season started in Europe and that helped develop the bond we had off the ice. I had a great season, personally, and the team was unbelievable. It was a dream come true. It was the type of thing you dream about when you were a little kid. It was the greatest year of my life.

"It is everyone's goal to be a winner and a Stanley Cup champion, but to be able to do that in the city of Boston made it even sweeter. It wasn't just the Bruins' history but what all the Boston teams were doing at the time. There is nothing better than to be a part of that team."

We've already established that Bruins fans and the team's tough guys have a special relationship. Players like Shawn Thornton, P.J. Stock, Jay Miller, and Milan Lucic are revered by fans long after they leave the organization. But if you add a Stanley Cup title to the resume, as both Thornton and Lucic did, that admiration increases exponentially. Those guys never have to buy a beer or a meal in Boston ever again—even though they can certainly afford to.

Each year, every player on the Stanley Cup–winning team gets his own personal day with the Cup, a tradition that dates back to 1995 with the New Jersey Devils. For Lucic, that meant bringing the Cup back to his hometown of Vancouver, just a month or so after the emotional series between the Bruins and Canucks that resulted in rioting in Vancouver after Game 7. Lucic considered all of that when it was his turn with the Cup.

"When I had my day with the Cup, I definitely didn't want to rub it in the faces of Canucks fans," Lucic said. "That's why we kept almost all of it private, with family and friends. We first brought the Cup to the Archangel Michael Serbian Orthodox Church in Burnaby, then we did a little boat cruise, to kind of keep it private…people aren't going to be jumping on and off the boat! We did the party up at Grouse Mountain so we could keep control of the people getting in as well. We wanted to keep it between me, my family, and my friends."

Lucic kind of chuckles at the idea that the greatest moment of his professional career had to be at the expense of the town and team he grew up rooting for.

"Honestly, I don't think it really made a difference," he said. "It was good because my family got to come to the games and not have to travel anywhere. I got to win the Cup in my hometown in an arena I grew up dreaming of playing in. But there was *some* bad with the aftermath of our Cup win and the rioting that went on in Vancouver. And some of the fans stayed around after we won the Cup, and many of those gave me the hometown boy cheer when it was my turn to skate with the Cup. I'm always grateful and thankful for that."

Despite the fact that he won a Memorial Cup and a Stanley Cup, Bruins fans think of one thing when they think of Lucic. It was one collision during one meaningless regular season game between the Bruins and Buffalo Sabres on November 12, 2011. Lucic ran into Sabres goaltender Ryan Miller, who had come out from his net to play the puck.

"I blocked a shot, and I pushed the puck ahead a little bit and saw that I had a bit of a breakaway," Lucic said. "But I ended up pushing it further ahead than I wanted to, so I was skating as hard as I could to get to the puck before Ryan Miller could get to it. I looked up once, and he was still in his net, then I looked back up again just outside the blue line and he was still back in his crease. When I looked up a third time, he was out of his net. It was just one of those reaction kinds of plays where you just kind of follow through. I guess I got a really good piece of him, although it wasn't my full intention to run the goalie. I guess he got hurt on the play. The league held a hearing and said all I deserved was the two-minute penalty.

"I *was* a little surprised that more Sabres players didn't come after me. I know that if the reverse had happened, and Tuukka [Rask] had been barreled into, guys on our team would have lined up for the chance to respond."

Lucic is right. The NHL said the two-minute minor penalty assessed to Lucic was sufficient punishment for the infraction involved. Miller disagreed and called Lucic "a piece of s—t" after the game. Miller was initially diagnosed with a concussion but later said he suffered a neck injury. He missed a number of games after the collision.

Lucic fought 13 times during the regular season of his rookie year. That number dropped to 11 his second year and has fallen pretty consistently ever since. He is still a willing combatant, but he has found it harder and harder to find other players willing to step up.

"By that point in my career, the word on the street and my reputation was that it was better to let the bear sleep," Lucic said. "When I would get angry and get physically engaged, the better I would play, and I could take over a game at times. Guys were definitely staying away from me more and more. Oh, I fought mad—sure! I don't know if it helped me or not, but I would say I'm scarier if I'm fighting mad!

"I'm similar to Terry [O'Reilly] in that I *do* have a switch on the ice. He and I are both Geminis with that twin or split personality. I'm also similar to Terry in that I like to think I'm nice and gentle and kind—off the ice—but when I flip that switch and the other side comes out, things can happen."

There certainly have been times when Lucic has felt the overall wear and tear of being a physical force in the National Hockey League, but he can remember only a couple of times when he was hurt in a fight.

"The first time I fought Jim Erskine, he hurt me pretty good," Lucic said. "Then that time I fought Colton Orr, he got me right in the nose and he broke it. I couldn't breathe out of my right nostril for a year and a half until I got it fixed. Those were the two who really hurt me. I'm so lucky and fortunate that my body has held up. Other than some broken knuckles and hands, as far as fighting is concerned, I wouldn't take it back for anything."

On June 26, 2015, Lucic's Bruins tenure came to an end. He was traded to the Los Angeles Kings for a first-round draft choice (which became Jakub Zboril), goaltender Martin Jones, and defenseman Colin Miller. He wasn't totally surprised that the Bruins were going to shake things up in that offseason.

"We missed the playoffs for the first time since I was in Boston," Lucic said. "It was kind of an up-and-down season, and then GM Peter Chiarelli got fired, so you didn't really know what was going to happen. I was going into a contract year, and there really weren't any talks leading up to that point.

"There was a lot going on my life at that time too. Two months before the trade, my dad passed away, and a month after that my second daughter was born, then a month after that I was traded to the Kings. There was a *lot* going on! But everything happens for a reason, and I'm just grateful and thankful I had the time I did have there in Boston. But going to L.A. with Dean Lombardi and Daryl Sutter was also awesome."

The following summer, Lucic signed as a free agent with the Edmonton Oilers, and then the unthinkable happened—a trade between the Oilers and their archrival, the Calgary Flames. It would be like the Boston Red Sox and New York Yankees or the Boston Bruins and Montreal Canadiens making a major deal. *And* Lucic had to waive his no-trade rights to even allow the deal to happen.

"I was playing for Edmonton, and my agent called and said Calgary was interested in trading for me," Lucic said. "I was thinking there is no way I'm waiving my no-trade clause to go to the Oilers' bitter rival. Then I have a couple of conversations with people, and later I spoke with Jarome Iginla about what it's like to play in Calgary. The Flames GM, Brad Treliving, said they really wanted me, so my wife and I decided we were just going to do it.

"I had five fights with the Calgary Flames when I was with the Oilers, but when I went to Calgary none of the guys I had fought were there. I guess that made it easier."

Lucic has now played more than 1,100 games in the NHL, and he's earned his reputation as one of the league's most-feared tough guys. He tries to keep up with the current crop of physical players in the league, but he also understands there is nowhere near the number of fighters in the league now as there was when he first arrived.

"When I came into the league there were three or four guys who could fight on almost every team," Lucic said. "Now, on most teams there might be just one.

"I used to study tough guys a lot more when I was younger, just because I had a lot more time. But now with three kids, I just don't have the same amount of time. I've always gone on Hockey Fights and watched other guys. Now with social media, I just follow them on Instagram and see all the fights as they come."

Lucic is one of those rare professional hockey enforcers— a guy teams prefer to stay away from. That has also led some to express disappointment that Lucic, by his own admission, is a much better player when he is physically engaged. I've seen him play when he was basically an unstoppable force. It was like watching NBA players trying to corral Shaquille O'Neal when he was completely engaged. Lucic is so big, and so strong, that there is just nothing you can do. But he has also gotten more than 100 penalty minutes only three times in his 16-year career. To put his career in perspective, Lucic had 56 fights in 566 games with the Bruins over eight seasons. In his eight seasons after leaving Boston, through 2022–23, he played in 607 games with just 33 fights. That's a pretty dramatic drop-off by any measure.

In free agency in 2023, Lucic returned to Boston for the 2023–24 season.

Lucic had thought a lot over the years about a possible return to Boston. When the signing was announced, Lucic made clear where his heart was.

"I was born and raised in Vancouver, but I feel like I really became an adult in Boston and really became a Bostonian. I missed being a Bruin more and more as the years went on. I found myself watching Bruins games. I caught myself cheering for the Red Sox, cheering for the Celtics, cheering for the Patriots.

"It's a place that's close and dear to my heart. Having the opportunity to come back, you can see the smile on my face right now. It feels like I'm going home. I've always felt like I've been a Bruin, and I'm just so happy and thankful for the opportunity to be a Bruin again."

Like so many others in this book and in professional hockey, Milan Lucic is exactly as advertised—a gentle giant, but *not* someone to mess with. As he says, better to let the bear sleep.

CHAPTER 5

DAVE BROWN

A NY NATIONAL HOCKEY LEAGUE franchise has had its share of tough guys. But it's safe to say there may not be an NHL team with *more* legitimate fighters over its history than the Philadelphia Flyers. The Flyers celebrate the nickname Broad Street Bullies and revere the men who have fought for the uniform over their history. This is a franchise that, at various times in its history, has had players like Todd Fedoruk, Dan Kordic, Donald Brashear, Craig Berube, Behn Wilson, and Dave Schultz wreaking havoc in arenas throughout North America.

I began my own career working for the Maine Mariners, the Flyers' minor league franchise located in Portland, Maine. Even at the AHL level, the Flyers were stocked with legendary battlers, many of whom moved on to drop the gloves for the parent team. In Maine, the Mariners fans loved fighters like Dave Hoyda, Jim Cunningham, Mike Busniuk, Glen Cochrane, John Paddock, Mel Hewitt, and Daryl Stanley. But the man who broke the AHL penalty-minute record in his rookie season and went on to a 14-year career in the NHL is considered by many to be the biggest and baddest of all the Flyers. Opposing players likely would not argue that the guy they least liked to fight was right wing Dave Brown.

The Flyers drafted Brown in the seventh round (140th overall) in the 1982 NHL entry draft. The 6'5", 210-pound Brown was born in Saskatoon, Saskatchewan, the son of Eleanor and Phillip. Dave has an older brother, Clint, and a sister, Tammie. He also knew at a very young age that if he wanted to continue to play hockey, there was one skill that he could take advantage of.

"Even at a young age, I knew that fighting was part of the game," Brown said. "I got kicked off my midget team, so at the age of 15 or 16 I was playing Junior B, and you had to fight even in that league. I knew from the start that if I was going to play, I was probably going to have to have fighting at least as a part of my game."

Even as a 15- or 16-year-old, Brown showed a willingness to stick up for a teammate, a quality he never lost even after playing in more than 700 NHL games. It is just part of his DNA to protect the players around him—even from his own coach.

"There was a kid on the midget team, and his parents never came to the games at all," Brown recalled. "The coach kind of favored another player over this kid, and I kind of spoke out. I said it wasn't fair that they cut this one kid, and the coach told me I had to apologize to the team. I said I wasn't going to do that, just because I felt what the coach did to the first kid was wrong. This kid was kind of on his own, and his parents weren't there to help him, so I spoke out, and they kicked me off the team when I was 15 years old.

"So I went to play Junior B hockey and at that time a team could have six players who were 20 or older. It was kind of a big step going from playing against 15-year-olds to playing against 20-year-old men.

"The Junior B team I played for was actually a pretty tough team, so I learned quickly that you had to take care of yourself. Even at that level, things were pretty rugged. You had to fight there, and you had to take care of yourself. I can remember a time when a guy knocked me down and when I got back up, he already had his gloves off! He kind of got the better of me that time, so a little later I kind of slashed him across the tops of his hands, and I think I might have broken his thumb. He never came around me again."

Those were wild days in junior hockey, and the game was certainly not for the faint of heart. Brown was bigger than most, and more willing than most, so he had no problems adjusting to the Western Hockey League. Brown got his chance to play for his hometown Saskatoon Blades.

"Even as far back as junior hockey, if you didn't have a tough team then your skills guys would be getting run by the other team continuously," Brown said. "You would have to have five or six tough guys—heavyweight guys—on most teams, just to take care of your players. The physical element was very prevalent. A lot of teams at that level would come in and just try to intimidate you. If you couldn't stand up to those teams, then your skill players, your top two lines, couldn't play the game. They were getting run all night.

"In Saskatoon we had a really tough team, so our skill guys didn't have a problem," Brown added.

Just how tough? That Blades team had the following penalty minute leaders in 1981–82: Bruce Gordon (353 PIM), Leroy Gorski (350 PIM), Dave Brown (344 PIM), and Donn Clark (257 PIM). The team had 13 players with more than 100 PIM.

It stands to reason that in the NHL draft following that season, Brown was hoping to hear his name called—and in his heart, he hoped his name would be called by Philadelphia.

"Maybe I was meant to be a Flyer," Brown said. "I remember growing up and liking the Broad Street Bullies, and a lot of those guys are from where I grew up. Dave Schultz was from Rosetown, Orest Kindrachuck was from Saskatoon, Don Saleski was from Saskatchewan. My grandma used to groom Ed Van Imp's poodle in the summer. So I always kind of felt a little connection to the Flyers, I guess.

"But I used to like the Bruins growing up, too. I would go into the barber shop, and they would put you up on the board to make you a little taller, and I would tell the barber, "I want that Bobby Orr haircut!" My Dad used to like the Bruins too because at that time they were one of the only teams that could beat Montreal, and Dad hated the Canadiens!"

After being drafted by the Flyers, Brown began his professional career with the Maine Mariners. It took no time at all for Brown to make a name for himself.

"We had a pretty tough squad my rookie season there in Portland," Brown said. "That was a big part of our success. We could go in and intimidate some teams. I had 418 penalty minutes that season, then another 107 in the Calder Cup playoffs. You get above 500 minutes in penalties for the year, you're working some. I broke the record that season with the 418, but not by much. I was mainly trying to establish myself in pro hockey, but I think in the back of my mind I was trying to break that penalty minute record too. I have to say that out of my whole pro career, that was one of the most fun seasons I ever had."

Brown was rewarded with a two-game call-up by the Flyers, and the team wanted to make sure he had a veteran presence available to show him the ropes. His first NHL roommate was all-time Flyers legend and future Hall of Famer, team captain Bobby Clarke. Brown remembers getting some pregame advice from Clarke before the team played the Boston Bruins on March 12.

"Clarkie didn't like Mike Milbury, and he was telling me I needed to grab Milbury and tune him up a little bit," Brown recalled. "But I had a thing going back to juniors with Gord Kluzak, so Gord ended up being my first NHL fight in my first game, not Milbury. I didn't think I did anything too bad to him, but I guess he had to be checked out at the hospital after. He was my size, and he was *tough!*"

In a Philadelphia radio interview years later, Milbury said he was just fine with Brown fighting Kluzak instead of him. As he told the interviewer, "Who wants to just get rag-dolled on the ice by a guy that big and strong?!"

Brown's fight with Kluzak was the first of 113 with the Flyers over two stints in Philadelphia and 142 total in his career, later with Edmonton and San Jose.

Brown earned 19 NHL games as a 21-year-old in his second season and made the move to stay in the 1984–85 season. But he also knew full well that *staying* at the NHL level was going to be even harder than getting there to begin with.

"Let's just say when I got up to Philadelphia, I was a border-line player. So the more I could contribute with what I *could* do, the better chance I had to stay there," Brown said. "The first thing was to make sure that no one bothered your team. And if there were any tough guys that wanted to fight you, then you had to fight them. Most important, though, was just reading the game. For instance, if we got down two goals early in the first period, you probably had to go out and try and change the momentum. I had to learn to read the game and do what I could do to make it better for our players. It wasn't necessarily fighting every game, but doing whatever was necessary to help your team win the game."

During Brown's career with the Flyers, two incidents stand out. Not surprisingly, both incidents involved fights, one of which earned Brown a 15-game suspension.

The Flyers had always had a heated rivalry with the New York Rangers. One player on the Rangers who really got under Brown and his teammates' skin was right wing Tomas Sandstrom.

"He was hurting our players," Brown said. "He was always sticking Mark Howe and sticking Ron Hextall. It was dirty—he was always slashing our guys."

Sandstrom's dirty play continued for several seasons, Brown said, and on several occasions, Brown tried to handle the situation.

"I remember the year before I hit him in the head, I speared him one time, but I didn't get caught. Then I speared him another time and got caught and earned a five-game suspension. His crap had been going on for a couple of years. I was frustrated that the league wouldn't stop him from doing it. You ask a lot of players, and a lot of people thought he was a dirty player. And he knew it!

"When it finally came down to it, and I finally hit him in the head, it came from a long period of trying to get him to stop what he had been doing. I really thought that the league should have cracked down on him, and it might not have come to that.

"Finally, I had just had enough. And when it happened, I didn't hit him as hard as I could have hit him. I could have really hurt him, and I didn't, but I think I scared him. It was a culmination of events, and I just had had enough. He ran into Hextall, and I snapped."

When Brown snapped, he cross-checked Sandstrom across the face right in front of the Flyers net and Ron Hextall. Sandstrom suffered a broken jaw and a concussion, and Brown was handed a 15-game suspension from the NHL.

"But I don't regret doing what I did," Brown said. "I was a guy who was supposed to take care of our team, and I felt that's what I did. Obviously, it was a reaction. It wasn't planned, but I hit him. It wasn't right, but I did it and I owned up to it."

Of course, that also made Brown a marked man every time he stepped into Madison Square Garden from that day forward. After serving his suspension and on his return to MSG, a fan unfurled a large bedsheet during the national anthem that read, DAVE BROWN—EAT S—T AND DIE! After the Flyers' victory that night against the Rangers, Brown told the media, "I guess Dave Brown eats s—t and wins!"

Brown was a huge part of another incident that helped change the game of hockey. It was the night before a playoff game against the Montreal Canadiens, and the two teams didn't have a *bench-clearing* brawl—they had a *dressing-room-clearing* brawl during pregame warm-ups. It was the brawl that changed the sport and banned that kind of thing forever.

Brown remembers vividly what happened that night on May 14, 1987, and what sparked the nearly 40-minute fracas. It all really began because of superstition. Claude Lemieux liked to be the final player off the ice and to put the puck into the opposing team's empty net before heading off.

In Game 4 of the series, Flyers backup goaltender Glenn "Chico" Resch foiled Lemieux by putting the net up against the boards at the end of the warm-up, and standing by it until Lemieux left the ice, frustrated. The Flyers won Game 4, so Resch decided the Canadiens would never put the puck into their empty net again.

"They somehow thought that gave them a mental edge or something," Brown said. "Eddie Hospodar just said, 'We're going to put an end to this.'

"We had all left the ice after warm-ups and Lemieux and Corson jumped back on the ice to put the puck in our net. Eddie and Chico Resch went back out there and confronted them, and Hospodar started punching out Lemieux. The Canadiens came out of their dressing room, and we came out of our dressing room too! It was on! I think that brawl with the Canadiens is one of the things I've been asked about the most."

The two Flyers players who went back on the ice to confront Lemieux had little to lose. Hospodar never played and was dressed only for warm-ups for the series. Resch was the veteran backup to Ron Hextall, who was the real reason the Flyers went as far as they did. So it was left to Hospodar and Resch to address what they felt was the disrespect shown by Lemieux and

Corson. The combatants later admitted that they really felt the altercation was a bit ridiculous, and both Lemieux and Resch said they were ready to let things go. But the Montreal Forum crowd was in full throttle, and when the Canadiens exited their dressing room en masse, it escalated quickly. Brown and his Flyers teammates were actually unaware of what was taking place out on the ice.

"Jim 'Turk' Evers, the Flyers' equipment manager, raced into the dressing room and said, 'Hey, they're fighting out there!' So we all just said, 'Let's go!' That thing went on for like 30 or 40 minutes.

"I got out on the ice and all I had on was a rib protector, because I had been having problems with my ribs. I used to go in the room after warm-ups and take off my sweater, my elbow pads, and my shoulder pads just to cool off. As I was running back onto the ice, I was trying to pull my elbow pads back on in case I fell on the ice."

Players from both teams sprinted onto the ice in similar states of undress. Doug Crossman had removed his skates and was wearing shower shoes. Chris Nilan said he had to put his skates back on and didn't even get them tied properly in his haste to join his teammates.

There was never a doubt what would be the main event in the brawl on the ice. Brown sought out Nilan, but he didn't have to look very hard because Nilan was looking for him too. The two fought for almost 10 minutes, and at one point in an exhausted clinch Brown asked Nilan if he had had enough. Nilan responded with a stinging right hand, and the two reengaged. Nilan admitted he had virtually nothing left in the tank for the rest of the game.

Back in the Flyers' dressing room, Hextall quickly did up the final strap on his pads and headed for the door to join his team on the ice. Coach Mike Keenan came in at that moment, closed the door, and stood in front of it, refusing to let the hotheaded Hextall join the brawl. Keenan feared his top goalie could get hurt—or suspended—before the Stanley Cup Final series. Brown thought Keenan did the right thing.

"I've got to give Keenan credit. He closed the door and locked it and wouldn't let Hexie get involved. Hexie was banging on the door and screaming, '*Let me out! Let me out!*' But Keenan wouldn't let him leave."

The Flyers got a third-period goal from Rick Tocchet to break a 3–3 tie and give the team a 4–3 win that propelled them to the Final. Hextall made 29 saves to get the win and in fact was named Conn Smythe Trophy winner as playoff MVP despite playing for the team that lost the Cup.

The aftermath of the incident that gave the entire NHL a black eye was remarkably understated. Hospodar was suspended for the Stanley Cup Final but would never have played anyway. There was a total of $24,500 in fines administered—a pittance even back in 1987. But the brawl also forced the league to take a long look at itself, and within months prohibitive individual and team punishments were put in place that ensured there would never be a repeat of that May night again.

For almost everyone involved with the sport, the pregame brawl between the Flyers and the Canadiens was an embarrassment. Even Don Cherry, well known for his celebration of fighting and the men who did it, admitted it made the NHL look bad. For people who enjoyed fighting in the NHL, it was fun but perhaps went a step too far. For people who knocked the NHL for fighting and brawling, it just affirmed what they already believed. But for anyone who has watched it—it's available on YouTube—it was amazing and frightening at the same time.

Brown always felt it was the first step that led the game to where it is today. He felt that the league had to clean up its image if it ever wanted to appeal to a broader national audience, and he even admits it probably was for the best.

Of course, the other big name involved in that incident, off the ice, was Keenan, a polarizing figure wherever he has coached, even after he won a Stanley Cup title with the New York Rangers. Keenan had a well-deserved reputation for picking on certain players, and Brown acknowledged that Keenan did that with the Flyers as well.

"Mike didn't bother me much," Brown said. "He got on a lot of guys and thought that was going to get them to play. He really had Doug Crossman square in his sights. Some guys dealt with it better than others, but Doug didn't like it. He didn't bother me much, because I mostly did my job. He very seldom said too much to me.

"We had some pretty good teams, and we kind of dealt with it within the team better than some guys might have dealt with it individually. Mark Howe and Brad McCrimmon were really good players, and they could handle it. Some other guys he really got to. As he usually did, Keenan eventually wore out his welcome with us too.

"In 1987, when we were going to the Final, I felt like Mike had to lay off on us and just let us play the game. We had a grind-it-out team already, but he was still just pushing and pushing. I honestly think we might have had a better chance if he had just laid off, but he would just keep it up. But Mike could definitely take it over the top, and he did with us and, like always, wore out his welcome. It was four years and he was done."

I had my own experience with Mike Keenan years later when he was coaching the Boston Bruins. Keenan took exception to something I said during the play-by-play of a subpar Bruins performance (and there were a lot of them that season) and started screaming during a team meeting that he was going to see that I was fired. I was warned about Keenan's tantrum by equipment man Peter Henderson and nervously contacted Nate Greenberg, the Bruins' assistant to the president, to see if my NHL career was in jeopardy. Nate calmly said, "Dale, you'll be here longer than he will be." As always, Nate was right.

The life of an NHL tough guy is a difficult one, and as Jay Miller has said, you're not allowed to have a night off. Brown admits it is something that can wear on a player at times.

"Sometimes you would sit in the dressing room and look at the game notes and think about who you might have to tangle with that night," Brown said. "On most teams there were one or two guys who you felt you might have to meet up with, but it didn't always play out like you might have planned. Some nights we might get up two or three goals fairly early, and I would just sit back and watch the game...handle things if something came up, but don't go looking for it.

"If you got down a couple of goals, you might change things up in the game. But there were many times when you would look at the other team's roster and you would know there was someone you were going to fight with. Sometimes,

I didn't even have to look at the roster; I already knew who those guys were."

Brown also said the position of enforcer has changed over the years. He knows players often talk before fighting, almost seeking permission for what is about to come. It wasn't always like that.

"Back then, guys didn't necessarily ask other guys to go with them," Brown said. "You wouldn't have to say anything, you would just go and do it. Now, guys ask each other if they want to fight, but when I played it wasn't really like that. Once in a great while, you might get the question asked, but usually you just kind of knew it. Often it was more of a reaction type of thing. Maybe you finished a check on a guy, and he wouldn't like it, so we would just fight.

"Back then, you had to be ready at any time. A lot of times, guys would just start on you before you were even ready. And I guess it could be the other way around too. But if it was a certain guy on the other team, if you even just ran into each other, you were probably going to have to fight."

A common theme among most of the tough guys I've talked to is that they don't generally feel they've been seriously hurt doing what they do. To quote the Toby Keith song, "It's a tough way to make an easy living," and sometimes you feel the pain.

"I remember I was fighting this guy in Portland one night— I'm pretty sure it was Bennett Wolf of the Baltimore Skipjacks— and I was hitting him," Brown said. "Then he kind of bull-rushed me, and it threw my helmet off the back of my head, and I hit my head on the ice. I remember asking the linesman to help me get up. I was half knocked out because I had smashed the back of my head on the ice. I sat on the bench the rest of the game.

"Later in my career, the hardest I ever got hit in a fight was against Billy Huard. We were playing an exhibition game against Ottawa, and I probably wasn't ready for him like I should have been. We squared off, but I wasn't really ready to fight. Our team had come out slow in the game, and I thought I had to do something to kind of wake us up. He hit me with a left hand right underneath my right eye, and that was the hardest I ever got hit in a fight. I can say I was pretty lucky as far as getting hurt is concerned. I never really got hurt too badly in a fight."

Some players refuse to consider the possible long-term toll this line of work has taken—or will take—on them. Perhaps they are afraid of talking it into existence. But Dave is one of the players who *has* at least thought about it.

"I may be a little bit concerned about head trauma and CTE," Brown said. "There are things I forget that are from a long time ago, but I think my dad has been the same way. I worry maybe a little bit, but not too much. I don't seem to have many short-term memory problems. I don't seem to have any mental problems. Look, if you make your living the way I did, I would have to say I'm a little concerned, but not to the point where I worry about having too many problems down the road. Hopefully not!

"But there are certainly times when I wonder if it's normal to not remember things back 20 years ago, and I've got a lot of stuff to remember, but I'm not sure…. Hopefully, the more important things will stay in there. There are always concerns because, let's face it, we were hit in the head a lot."

But even tough guys can occasionally find humor in their line of work. Brown has a humorous anecdote involving another subject of this book—legendary enforcer Archie Henderson.

"Archie didn't have very good hearing, and he might have even played with hearing aids or something," Brown said. "We were playing against him in New Haven, and I was back checking on the play while Daryl Stanley was backing in on the play, playing defense. Archie was on the rush for New Haven, and he went offside. Daryl yelled at him, and said, 'You're offside!' Archie wasn't looking straight at him when he said that, so he knew Stan was saying something to him, but he didn't know exactly what it was. Archie looked at him a second time, and Daryl yelled again, 'You're offside!' Archie thought Stan was calling him out, so he just responded, 'All right! Let's go, then!' So away they went! All because Archie was just offside!"

Like all NHL tough guys, Brown keeps a checklist in his head. He knows who the other tough guys were and remembers which were hardest to deal with.

"I can't really say any one player in particular was tougher on me than any other, because there were a lot of guys who were tough," Brown said. "I think Jay Miller was one of the guys I fought the most, and he was always tough. Stu Grimson was really tough too. Bob Probert, obviously, was very, very tough. Marty McSorley was tough. There were a lot of guys.

"There was an era after I finished up playing when the guys got really, really big. I played at 210 or 215 pounds, but guys were coming up like Jody Shelley, Colton Orr—these guys were a little bit bigger than everybody else. Shelley probably played at like 235. Chris Simon was in that group too. That was a tough era.

"Even when Shawn Thornton was fighting in that era, he was fighting a lot of much bigger guys. You have to give him credit for fighting a lot of guys who were bigger and heavier than he was."

Even tough guys like Brown had to learn, as their careers went forward, that there are rules to follow amid the mayhem. Guys like that rely on those rules to keep some order in the disorder.

"Most guys who play the way I did have a code of some sort," Brown said. "There are certain things you try to live by. You knew that if there was a young guy coming up on the other team, you were probably going to have to fight him. You would give him a chance. You didn't sucker anybody. If you followed certain rules, you got respect because of that.

"By the time I went back to play for the Flyers the second time, I was probably a little more selective about who and when I would fight. At that stage of my career, I didn't think it was necessary to fight every night. If our team was playing well, and we were doing okay, I didn't think I had to accept every challenge that was thrown out there."

Brown is currently the head of pro scouting for the Philadelphia Flyers. Part of his job is to assess the players throughout the league and see what works and what doesn't. He certainly understands that there have been changes in the sport over the years, and he doesn't necessarily like all of them.

"In today's game, you just don't have enough tough guys anymore," Brown said. "I think the game would be better today if we had more toughness in it. Before, players could settle some things amongst themselves, but nowadays all the pressure is on the referees to call every single penalty. I think there's still a place for fighting and for physical play in the game. I think the game suffers when you have less and less of that.

"There are a lot of players playing the game today who could not have played back in our era. You had to bring some toughness with you when you played then, and not everyone who plays now has that in them."

Tough guys did play with some fear, but not the fear you might expect. They almost never feared the physical confrontation—in fact, they often sought that out. It was a completely different fear that drove Dave Brown and many other players like him.

"The worst thing I could have ever imagined was if I went into the dressing room after the game and my teammates thought I didn't do my job," Brown said. "That was always going through my head and was the worst feeling, so I would do whatever it took to help my team. It was the pressure of doing the best job you could at whatever the team needed you to do. If at the end of the game, my teammates thought I had done my job, that was good enough for me."

Even among NHL tough guys, certain players are spoken about almost in reverence. Dave Brown seems to be one of those guys. His size, determination, and willingness to play the game at that level and never back down are laudable.

Brown had 113 fights in 552 games over two stints with the Flyers. He fought 27 times in 140 games with the Edmonton Oilers and two more times in 37 games with the San Jose Sharks. And his last fights ever in the NHL? He fought with Todd Ewen of the Anaheim Ducks in the first period of a game on March 31, 1996, and followed it up with a heavyweight tussle with Ken Baumgartner later in the same period. His final fight ended when Brown lifted Baumgartner and tossed him over the boards and into the Ducks bench. Heavyweight champions like Dave Brown end their fighting careers much like they started them—making a statement.

CHAPTER 6

JOHN SHANNON

———

I HAVE HAD THE HONOR and privilege of working in professional hockey for more than 40 years. I have met and become friends with managers, players, coaches, trainers, equipment men, broadcasters, and others who work behind the scenes in hockey. When I wanted to add the perspective of a longtime broadcaster and broadcast executive to this book, the first name that came to mind was John Shannon.

Shannon was a panelist on Rogers Sportsnet's Hockey Central and also won an Emmy for his work for NBC at the Salt Lake City Winter Olympics. In 2008 he was named executive in charge of programming and production for NHL Network, and was the executive vice president of programming and production for the NHL. In the interest of full disclosure, John also served as a regular on our pregame Bruins coverage on New England Sports Network (NESN). There is little in the domain of radio and television coverage of the NHL that John does *not* know. Naturally, I wanted to get his input on this topic as well.

We started our conversation with my assertion that hockey players, in general, are easy to deal with, but hockey tough guys may be the most approachable of all hockey players.

"I think that's fair. The non-stars across the board in our game are the most approachable," Shannon said. "They love the game so much, they love to talk the game and they love to be a part of the game. It's only in recent times that we started to see superstars hired to become analysts and television announcers. For the longest time, it was always the fringe players, the fighters and guys like that. They were the ones who loved to talk about the game and loved to entertain. It was easy for them to do that.

"The third- and fourth-line guys were more fun to talk to, and fighters were usually in that group. Shawn Thornton is a great example of that kind of guy. Would you rather go out and have a beer with Shawn Thornton or Patrice Bergeron? A lot of people would say that Thornton would be a lot more fun. But I've never been out for a beer with either of them."

It is obvious that there has been a dramatic decline in NHL fighting over the years. Most feel that it's something that the powers in the league offices want to happen. But Shannon observes, as many of us do, that fighting in the NHL is just not a primary topic anymore.

"It is certainly not the factor now that it was 20 years ago or 30 years ago," Shannon said. "I'm not sure the television partners in the NHL even have an opinion about fighting anymore...how to show the fights, how to describe the art of intimidation. It's funny, it's become such a small factor in the game today that I think now people are surprised when a fight occurs. As a result, they really don't know, in a lot of ways, how to cover it."

But television executives certainly knew how to cover fighting in earlier days. Fighting was much more prevalent—bench-clearing brawls included—until the late '80s. Everyone had to know exactly what they were supposed to do when the fighting started.

"I can tell you right now, from a television perspective, in those days we had an action plan when you felt there was the potential for a bench-clearing brawl. Our director could call out in just a couple of words to get in 'brawl mode.' He might say, 'Watch out for the benches,' and every camera had an assignment to ensure that we would know immediately and accurately who the first player off the bench was. We had a camera isolated on each bench and cameras on the coaches and cameras to isolate on the fights on the ice as they started. We had to be able to tell the complete story of the genesis of the brawl."

One of the more memorable brawls in the history of the league is chronicled in this book by the guys who were directly involved—Dave Brown of the Philadelphia Flyers and Chris Nilan of the Montreal Canadiens. The infamous pregame brawl before Game 7 of their Stanley Cup playoff series is generally credited with changing the culture of the sport. It was after that game that bench-clearing brawls were basically eliminated from the sport. But Shannon knew there was never a question that the brawl was going to be seen by the *Hockey Night in Canada* audience.

"In fact, on Canadian TV they *did* cover it," Shannon said. "They covered the whole thing, but they had to—they were given no choice. When I started, *Hockey Night in Canada* had a whole set of rules how to show fights. Obviously, you showed the fight live, punch by punch, and you could cover it like you were covering Ali–Frazier. But for the Canadian market, we never showed more than the first punch on the replay. You showed how the fight started, then you stopped. We had conditioned the viewers over a long period of time of the '70s and '80s that that's how it happened.

"Then we would go to Philadelphia or New York or Boston, and their local telecasts were totally different. Prism in Philly or MSG in New York or TV-38 in Boston would show the *whole* fight, replay-wise. As much as we were purists of the game, and understood the role of fighting, we were aghast that you would replay a whole fight. But it was philosophically different how to handle the aspect of showing fighting between Canada and the United States."

As infamous as that pregame brawl between the Flyers and Canadiens was, Shannon feels another brawl was even more violent and more graphic. The Canadiens were again involved (so much for those high-flying, skillful Canadiens!), but this time they were playing their province rivals, the Quebec Nordiques.

The two teams met in the second round of the 1984 Stanley Cup playoffs, so emotions were riding even higher than normal. After Montreal shut out the Nordiques 4–0 at Le Colisée in Game 5, they returned to the Forum with a chance to eliminate their archrivals. The game was played on April 20, 1984, and became known as *la bataille du Vendredi saint*—the Good Friday Massacre.

As the second period came to an end, a bench-clearing brawl broke out. There were 14 altercations in the brawl, including Mario Tremblay of the Canadiens smashing Peter Stastny in the nose and Quebec's Louis Sleigher sucker punching Jean Hamel and knocking him out. Referee Bruce Hood, in an attempt to calm things down, sent both teams to their respective dressing rooms before assessing the penalties.

As the two teams came back out for the third period, the public address announcer started reciting the litany of offenses. It was the first time the players learned that they had been given game misconducts from Hood and were tossed from the game. At that time, with many players thinking they had nothing to lose, another brawl broke out. That second brawl before the start of the third period featured a fight between Dale Hunter of the Nordiques and Mark Hunter of the Canadiens. You guessed it— Dale and Mark were brothers.

"Believe it or not," Shannon said, "worse than that Flyers/Canadiens pregame brawl was the Good Friday Massacre in 1987. It was at the end of the second period, and it was, by far, more violent than that Philly–Montreal brawl. You had to cover it, you had no choice but to cover it, and the severity of the fight was absolutely horrific.

"Hockey goes through cycles of calling for an end to fighting, and this was one of those cycles, but in the end we always seem to fall back on giving the fans what they want. The emotions of two teams can be so high, and hockey players play right to the edge, and sometimes they go over the edge and that's what happens."

I mentioned to Shannon that Harry Sinden had told me years ago that the NHL had to eliminate fighting if it ever hoped to appeal to a wider audience. It's fair to say Shannon wasn't necessarily buying what Harry was selling.

"By the way, I've known Harry for a long time and Harry always seemed to tailor his opinions depending on how tough the Bruins were," Shannon said. "The years the Bruins were tough, fighting had to stay in the game, and the moment the Bruins got a little softer, Harry thought we had to get rid of it.

"In the '70s, '80s, and early '90s, the 'Mandarins,' as I liked to call them—the general managers—had a lot more influence on how the game was officiated, how it was played. You could see all of these guys—Bill Torrey, Harry Sinden, Glen Sather, Lou Nanne, and a few more—would change their opinion based on who they had on their own rosters. Harry Sinden wouldn't have wanted players like Wayne Cashman, John Wensink, Stan Jonathon, Terry O'Reilly when he was the general manager? Come on, Harry!"

A man who has covered the NHL for as long as Shannon has seen his share of NHL tough guys. When prompted, he rattled off several right away.

"Dave Semenko comes to mind. If you look at his numbers, he didn't fight as much as people thought, but he was so intimidating that it often didn't get to that point," Shannon said. "What Dave Semenko did for the Edmonton Oilers became legendary. And when he did fight, it was scary! You mentioned Dave Brown— I'm not sure there was a tougher guy in the game than Dave Brown. Ever. Another guy, who has now become a lawyer, is Ken Baumgartner. Tough, tough, tough man! I might add Tim Hunter in Calgary. I had a front-row seat to the Hunter–Semenko rivalry, and it was a big part of the Battle of Alberta on a regular basis. Both of those guys were also great people—personable, funny, would always go out of their way to say hello. But when the switch got flicked, oh my goodness gracious!"

Shannon says Baumgartner was one of those players who truly refined the "art of intimidation":

"Baumgartner was famous for skating into scrums and saying, 'Hey, boys! Kenny's here!' And suddenly things would settle down. They knew that even though they thought they were tough, they didn't want to get into a fight with Ken Baumgartner."

Even coaches earn an honorable mention in the toughness department. Former Canadiens, Maple Leafs, and Bruins head coach Pat Burns was a police officer prior to his NHL career. Darryl Sutter is one of six famous Sutter brothers who played in the NHL, and they were all very tough customers.

On May 22, 1997, the Colorado Avalanche and Detroit Red Wings were playing Game 4 of the Western Conference finals at the Joe Louis Arena. The two teams had already been involved in an emotional and physical bout, dating back to the playoffs the previous season. Claude Lemieux checked Kris Draper from behind into the lip of the boards in front of the Red Wings bench, breaking Draper's jaw, cheekbone, and orbital bone. The Avalanche won that Game 6, eliminating the Red Wings, and went on to win the Stanley Cup.

The two teams played three times the following season without serious incident, but the fourth and final regular season meeting was on March 26, with the very real possibility the two teams would clash again in the upcoming playoffs. The game was a bloodbath, with 18 fighting majors and 148 minutes in penalties. The main event for the game was likely a full-fledged, masks-off brawl at center ice between goaltenders Patrick Roy and Mike Vernon. Detroit's Darren McCarty took advantage of the opportunity to gain a measure of revenge for his linemate Kris Draper. McCarty sucker-punched Lemieux, dragged him to the boards, and kneed him in the head before officials broke things up.

If you've seen the superb ESPN 30 for 30 documentary about this rivalry, *Unrivaled*, you saw McCarty and Lemieux live on stage in Detroit talking about the series and the aftermath. You also saw video of the two coaches, Detroit's Scotty Bowman and Colorado's Marc Crawford, seeming to try and get at each other at the bench area. John Shannon had been there to see it all as well and knew exactly what happened with the coaches.

"In that famous Detroit Red Wings–Colorado Avalanche bloodbath in the Stanley Cup playoffs, the great TV shot was of Scott Bowman jawing with Marc Crawford on the benches," Shannon said. "Scotty is such a brilliant s—t disturber; he always knows exactly what to say. Scotty was from Peterborough and Marc's dad was a coach for years and years in the Belleville area. Scotty was not yelling; he was just calmly saying to Marc Crawford, 'Your dad, Floyd, would be so disappointed.' And that caused Marc to just blow!"

A book focusing on NHL tough guys isn't necessarily limited to fighters or enforcers. Toughness takes many forms, and Shannon remembered a playoff story that involved former New York Rangers tough guy Nick Fotiu when he was a member of the Calgary Flames.

"There's a story from 1985, the Stanley Cup playoffs, Battle of Alberta, Calgary and Edmonton," Shannon began. "I think it was Game 3 or 4 in Calgary. Nick Fotiu goes into the corner and gets hit by a puck or a stick in the groin, and it crushes one of his testicles. And he *doesn't leave the ice!* He finishes the game! Overnight, he phones the doctor, and he says, 'I don't know what's wrong, but there's something going on here.' He had to go into surgery that night! Now, that's not fighting, but *that's tough!*"

I was there to witness what Bruins center Patrice Bergeron put himself through to play in the 2013 Stanley Cup Final against the Chicago Blackhawks. After the Bruins were eliminated by the Blackhawks in Game 6, Bergeron went directly to the hospital. We learned later that he had played in that game with a broken rib, torn rib cartilage, a separated shoulder, and a pinhole puncture in his lung. He played 24 shifts and was on the ice for 17:45.

His teammate, Zdeno Chara, became a Boston legend for what he played through in the 2019 Stanley Cup Final against the St. Louis Blues. In Game 4 of the series, Chara took a puck to the face. Injury details are always held tight to the vest, especially in the playoffs. Chara returned to the bench for the rest of Game 4, but it was also obvious he was in considerable pain. Little did we know.

When the series resumed in Boston for Game Five, the Bruins captain was introduced as part of the starting lineup—standing on the blue line for the national anthem wearing a huge, plastic, full-face cage. I've been through some exciting moments covering games at TD Garden but have never—*ever*—heard anything like the ovation Chara received that night.

After the Bruins were eliminated in Game 7, we learned what Chara had been playing through. His jaw was broken in two places—on the left and right sides of his face. The right side of his jaw was separated into two pieces and had to be held together by pins. He had plates on both sides of his face and his jaw was wired shut. He survived on a liquid diet to get through the final three games of the series, and his recovery took more than a month.

Again, the premise of this book is hockey tough guys, but that doesn't always mean fighting. Often it means just surviving.

"There are so many stories like that, so many players who play the game so injured," Shannon said. "The amount of pain that Bobby Orr endured with those prehistoric surgeries conducted on those knees, and what he put himself through. One of my best friends is John Davidson, and he played his last two years in the National Hockey League with no cartilage in either knee!

"Now, the game made Bobby famous, made him wealthy, and gave him connections to people. There are lots of positives out of it, but that day you can't get out of bed, I have to wonder if it's all worth it.

"How do you put yourself through that? I guess you love the game so much and you want to compete at the elite level. You want to fulfill your dream that you had as a child, no matter what country you came from, of playing in the National Hockey League. But at what price? I hope, when they get to their seventies and eighties, that they'll still think that it was worth it."

In the same way that Bobby Orr was an idol to me and so many others around New England, John had his own childhood hero, and he saw the toll the game took on him prior to his passing.

"I watch these guys play now, and they're in their twenties and thirties, but the guys who were that age when I *started* watching are now in their seventies and eighties," Shannon said. "My boyhood idol was Andy Bathgate. I loved Andy Bathgate! Two years ago, at the Hall of Fame event, I saw Andy and he could barely stand up. His back was gone, his knees were gone, and I'm thinking, 'Man, that's my idol!' I was thrilled to meet him, and when I told him he was my boyhood idol he smiled and said, 'Thank you.' But I saw him with a bad back and bad knees and his hands were riddled with arthritis, and you couldn't help but wonder if that price was worth it. They're the only ones that can answer that question."

John knows that toughness comes in many different forms and so does intimidation. The game is certainly different today than it used to be, and fighting is much less a part of its DNA. But toughness hasn't always been limited to the people who drop the gloves.

"On the other side were the great power forwards of our time," Shannon said. "Cam Neely was on that list, Brendan Shanahan, Clark Gillies. These guys were really tough, but they could also score. Make no mistake about it, if they were forced to be tough, they could be tough! Gordie Howe was probably the original power forward. Nobody fought Howe because they were scared of him! Howe was given so much room because he was so intimidating."

There have been several incidents over the years that have caused the NHL national embarrassment. Unfortunately for the league, the altercations were also on live television for all the world to see.

On February 21, 2000, the Bruins were playing the Canucks in Vancouver. During the game, Donald Brashear of the Canucks fought with Marty McSorley of the Bruins, and by most accounts Brashear won the fight handily. As the fight was broken up,

Brashear taunted the Bruins bench. Later in the game, Brashear collided with Bruins goaltender Byron Dafoe, who had to be taken from the ice on a stretcher with a knee injury. McSorley spent most of the rest of the game trying to fight with Brashear, who refused. With just 4.6 seconds remaining, McSorley struck Brashear with a two-handed slash on the right temple, knocking him unconscious.

McSorley was suspended indefinitely by the NHL and in fact never played another game. He was also charged with assault with a weapon and found guilty in a British Columbia courtroom.

On March 8, 2004, the Vancouver Canucks were hosting the Colorado Avalanche. The Canucks harbored hard feelings toward Steve Moore after he had injured their leading scorer, Markus Naslund, with a hit to the head in a game on February 16. Naslund suffered a minor concussion and a bone chip in his elbow, missing the next three games. Canucks head coach Marc Crawford criticized the game officials for the lack of a penalty call, and Vancouver forward Brad May issued a "bounty" on Moore. The two teams met on March 3 and Commissioner Gary Bettman attended, with no incidents in the game.

Five days later, they met again.

In the first period, Moore fought with Vancouver's Matt Cooke, earning a five-minute fighting major. Midway through the third period, and with the Avalanche leading 8–2, Colorado's Todd Bertuzzi was sent onto the ice and failed in several attempts to goad Moore into a fight. When Moore ignored him, Bertuzzi chased Moore from behind, grabbed his jersey, and punched him in the jaw, rendering him unconscious. Moore's head hit the ice, and Bertuzzi fell on top of him.

Moore lay on the ice for 10 minutes before being removed on a stretcher. He was taken to the hospital in Vancouver before being transferred to a Denver hospital. He was treated for three fractured vertebrae in his neck, ligament damage to his vertebra, facial lacerations, an injury to his brachial plexus nerves, and a grade-three concussion. He also had amnesia.

Bertuzzi was suspended for the remainder of the regular season and the upcoming Stanley Cup playoffs. The Attorney General's office in British Columbia charged Bertuzzi with assault causing bodily harm, and he faced as much as a year and a half in prison. He avoided jail time as a result of a plea deal and a guilty plea to the charge. Moore also filed several civil suits against Bertuzzi, the Canucks, Crawford, May, and others. Moore was not cleared to play medically and ultimately had to give up on several aborted comeback attempts.

Shannon certainly did not attempt to justify the actions of either Marty McSorley or Todd Bertuzzi, but he did try to understand them.

"Sometimes players who get to that line go over that line," Shannon said. "I think they just snap. I've never played the game, but I can tell you that sometimes players get so emotionally involved in the event that they cross the line. What Todd Bertuzzi did with Steve Moore was chase him back up the ice. If it wasn't Bertuzzi, it was probably going to be another Canuck player because they were so mad at him. Moore got jumped by Todd Bertuzzi, and it was unfortunate that he fell the way he did. But at that point, Bertuzzi wasn't really thinking straight.

"That whole Donald Brashear–Marty McSorley thing in Vancouver—Marty was in the wrong and felt that Brashear didn't respect the code. Marty will tell you he tried to put his stick on Donald's shoulder, but that's not what happened. We expect these guys to play controlled, but sometimes the best hockey is chaos!"

Another "tough guy" was celebrated in 2016 by hockey fans who took advantage of online voting and elected John Scott of the Arizona Coyotes captain of the Pacific Division team for the NHL All-Star game. Before the game could be played, however, the Coyotes traded Scott to the Montreal Canadiens, who then assigned him to their AHL affiliate, the St. John's Icecaps.

The NHL still allowed Scott to participate in the All-Star Game despite the fact that he was not even in the NHL at the time of the game and had just one assist for the season for Arizona at the time of his trade to Montreal. He completed his NHL career with a total of five goals and 544 penalty minutes.

Fans got their "gotcha" moment to embarrass the NHL; Scott celebrated that moment by scoring two goals in the tournament and was named MVP. One of the tough guys I spoke with for this book did not appreciate what Scott was allowed to do, and John Shannon was in complete agreement.

"Whoever you were talking to was bang-on," Shannon said. "To me, it created a sideshow. The All-Star Game should be a celebration of the elite in the game and the skill in the game. I don't know John Scott, and have never met him, but to me it was making a mockery of what the All-Star Game was all about. And I can tell you that most of my friends in the NHL office felt the same way."

Like so many people I spoke to in the process of writing this book, Shannon admits that his opinion of fighting in the game has changed over the years. He has looked at the long-term effects on the health of the players and the diminishing impact of fighting on the game to restate his thoughts on fighting in hockey.

"Over the years, my opinion of fighting in hockey has totally evolved," Shannon said. "I know the game can still be great without it. I was 40 feet away in the basket beside Danny Gallivan for the Pierre Bouchard and Stan Jonathan battle. I was right there. It was an eye-opening experience in so many ways, not just what was happening on the ice, but the reaction of the crowd. The reality is these guys, as competitors, will do anything it takes to win. I didn't mind a good fight every once in a while. I hated the staged fights and the need for every team to have a goon. I love the art of the game, but if I never see another hockey fight it will never bother me.

"I'm not speaking for Gary Bettman, or Bill Daly, or any of the owners or the players association when I say this, but you've got to be concerned about player safety. I almost think you've got to protect players from themselves. Getting rid of fighting may be one of those steps you need to consider. I do think the NHL is concerned for players."

I pointed out to Shannon that among the most fragile bones in the human body are the bones in the hands and fingers, and among the hardest bones in the body are those in the head. Whether that head is covered by a hard plastic helmet and face shield or not is also beside the point. The very idea of pounding a head or helmet with a bare knuckle can, at times, seem a little silly.

"Yes, it is, but it's also pugilism at its purest," Shannon said. "For some reason, in our society, we've always put fighters on a pedestal. Not necessarily in hockey, but when you think about the greatest fighters ever, why would you even consider boxers as heroes? Why do we do that? I don't get it sometimes. But people still love the art of hand-to-hand combat. There are days when we're not as civilized as we think we are."

So that brings up the larger philosophical question in hockey today. With fighting being diminished to a large extent and perhaps heading toward total elimination, is it possible to still play intimidating hockey?

"What did the St. Louis Blues do to the Boston Bruins in the Stanley Cup Final in 2019?" Shannon mused. "Would you define what the Blues did to the Bruins as intimidating hockey? I think how the Blues played against the Bruins is as close to what you would consider intimidating hockey in this day and age. Now, the Edmonton Oilers want to intimidate you in other ways. They want to intimidate with their speed, and if you take a penalty then they'll just kill you on the power play. The word *intimidation* has evolved. The days of using the body and fisticuffs is slowly being replaced by skill and speed. But that's still intimidating, and the moment you flinch, life is different.

"We've gone from those Big, Bad Bruins or Broad Street Bullies or New York Islanders teams to where we are today. Heck, the Islanders were an intimidating team in so many ways. They were physical, they were dirty, they would make you think, they were fast. Their goaltender [Billy Smith] was intimidating! He wasn't afraid of shaking that stick at anyone! Creating fear in the opposition is what you are trying to do, and the rules now make that difficult. Rule 48, hitting from the side, hits to the head, body checks from behind that were for the longest time legal aren't any more. That art of intimidation has changed.

"Remember—Connor McDavid has never played a game of NHL hockey in the clutch-and-grab world. That's forced a lot of change in the game!"

CHAPTER 7

CHRIS NILAN

THE MAN'S NICKNAME IS KNUCKLES, for God's sake! If you're on a first-name basis, maybe you get to call him Knucks. Either way, is there any doubt that Chris Nilan had to make this list as one of the toughest guys to have ever played the game?

Oh, and about that nickname? Even *that* is another Chris Nilan story.

"I had a couple of fights off the ice during my playing days at Northeastern, and it kept me from being *on* the ice," Nilan began. "I ended up with a couple of teeth embedded in my hand after a street fight. My friend Joe Mahoney took the teeth out of my hand with tweezers. He poured what must have been a full bottle of peroxide on it to clean it.

"The next day we had a game, and I couldn't get my hand in my hockey glove because it was so swollen. I was young and stupid and didn't understand anything. My hand got infected from a human bite wound and it got into my bloodstream. I ended up in the hospital and had two surgeries—one to clean it all up and put a wick in it, and the other one to take skin grafts from my hip to cover it up.

"Then I had another fight and broke my hand in a fight off the ice again. My hands were always cut up or something. And my teammate Gerry Dwyer just yelled, 'Knuckles! Look at those hands!' The guys just started calling me Knuckles and it stuck."

But let's not get ahead of ourselves. Like so many Massachusetts kids, Chris Nilan became a hockey player because of just one man—the incomparable Bobby Orr.

"Bobby Orr come to town, and they started putting up these MDC rinks all over the place, and they put one up on the end of my street in West Roxbury," Nilan said. "When Bobby came to town it just changed everything for Boston kids.

"I remember the first time I ever saw him play live at the Garden. I snuck in with a couple of friends, and we're sitting in the aisles. We would move around, but the ushers were pretty good about it too. I saw Bobby grab the puck behind the net and as he started up the ice, everybody stood up out of their seats. He skated through everybody, came down, and scored. The fan frenzy and how loud the Garden was—to witness that firsthand—made me think, 'Man, I would love to play this game someday! I would love to be a Boston Bruin!'

"I always admired their team toughness and the way they played the game. It certainly lined up with how I was growing up on the streets. The Bruins were a team that didn't take any crap from anyone, and I was kind of the same way."

Like a lot of Boston kids, Nilan's game started on the streets and moved into one of those MDC (Metropolitan District

Shawn Thornton has two Stanley Cup rings—one as a member of the Anaheim Ducks and the other with the Boston Bruins. He is considered one of the premier fighters of his era.

Terry O'Reilly's hockey skills were understated, sometimes even by him. In addition to his pugilistic prowess, "Taz" also made himself into a very good player.

But when most people think of Terry O'Reilly, this is likely the first vision that pops into their heads.

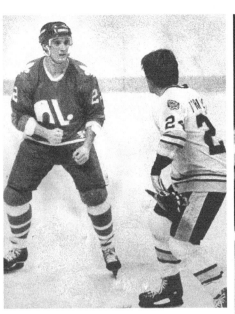

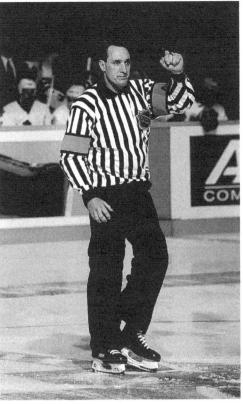

Paul Stewart made his NHL debut at the Boston Garden and fought three Bruins, earning a game misconduct. His first fight was against Terry O'Reilly. (David Hughes)

Ironically, Stewart moved onto a second career as a longtime NHL referee as well.

Don't let the professorial demeanor of coach Archie Henderson fool you. Archie the player was a legendary hockey enforcer. (© Ricky Rogers / The Tennessean, Nashville Tennessean via Imagn Content Services, LLC)

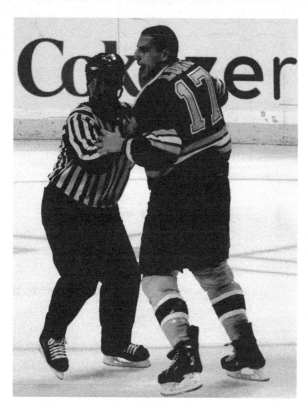

Milan Lucic walked around at a comfortable 235 pounds, making most opponents decide that leaving him alone was the best option. (David Hughes)

There have been few enforcers more feared than Dave Brown, shown here battling against Rob Ray of the Buffalo Sabres while playing for the Philadelphia Flyers.

John Shannon has had a long and storied career covering the National Hockey League and has seen some of the game's great battles.

Chris Nilan realized his boyhood dream of playing for his hometown Boston Bruins, but his greatest success came as a member of the Montreal Canadiens.

Jay Miller gained fame as a member of his hometown Boston Bruins but moved to the Los Angeles Kings when Wayne Gretzky needed a protector.

Mike Milbury was a member of the Big, Bad Bruins and followed the lead of people like his teammate Terry O'Reilly. (David Hughes)

Brian Burke brought his trademark truculence to the Anaheim Ducks and earned a Stanley Cup title in 2007.

Matthew Barnaby may have been a "middleweight" by hockey enforcer standards, but he was always willing to take on the game's heavyweights.

P.J. Stock was a fan favorite, mostly because of his fearless and relentless approach to playing the game. He was often willing take a few blows in order to land a big one of his own. (Patricia McDonnell/Associated Press)

Bobby Robins' fight with Luke Schenn in his NHL debut was likely the beginning of the end of Robins' career.

Commission) rinks that were sprouting up all over the commonwealth. I've often said that every MDC rink should be named after Bobby Orr, because they all came about due to his influence. The name has been changed from MDC to DCR (Massachusetts Department of Conservation and Recreation), but there are reportedly 42 of these rinks in the commonwealth. One is now called the Jim Roche Community Arena at 1275 VFW Parkway in West Roxbury, and that's where Chris started to learn his game.

"I played street hockey every chance I got and then I ended up going to that MDC rink that they built at the end of my street," Nilan said. "The Charlie Doyle League was the first league in West Roxbury, but before the league started, the rink was open for a solid year and I went up there *every* day after school. I paid my 25 cents for public skating, and I was there *all the time*. I wasn't even playing hockey; I was just skating that first year. Eventually the Doyle League came in, named for a local representative in the neighborhood, and he started the league. But from the day I played in my very first game I always wanted to be a Boston Bruin."

As is often the case, you need someone to take an interest in you to make your mark, and in Chris Nilan's case, that someone was Judge Paul King.

"I went from the Charlie Doyle League to Parkway to Hub City to play for my friend Judge Paul King and then on to Catholic Memorial High School," Nilan said. "I spent a year at Northwood Prep up in Lake Placid and then on to Northeastern University. Judge King was the guy who mentored me and was really responsible for helping me get into the NHL. Judge King's brother was the governor, Ed King."

I certainly wondered how a guy like Chris Nilan could play college hockey, where players are not allowed to fight. That did not seem to fit into how Nilan played the game, but he didn't think it was much of a problem.

"In college I certainly played aggressively, but I only had one fight in college," Nilan said. "We were up at Colgate, and I remember a kid named Larry Gibson. There was a controversy over a call. He was talking with the refs and our captain was also talking with the officials. I came in and said something and Gibson said something like, 'What are you even doing over here?' I ended up dropping him. I didn't even take my glove off, but I punched him with my glove on. It was the only fight I ever had in college hockey, and I got suspended and missed the second game of the Beanpot.

"You might think it was difficult for me to play college hockey, where you can't fight, but it wasn't that bad for me. I continued to play aggressively, but I just never fought because it wasn't allowed. Certainly, all the pushing and shoving and face washing went on, but the fighting didn't happen. But I also never aspired to be a fighter in the NHL. I knew when I got there I wasn't going to take any crap from anybody, but I wanted to play hockey. I wanted to score goals! I wanted to be a player."

What Nilan didn't know at the time was that Judge Paul King also had friends in high places—friends like Montreal Canadiens greats Dickie Moore and Doug Harvey.

"It wasn't until the Judge passed and I was at his funeral that I learned that he was friends with these famous Montreal

Canadiens," Nilan said. "I met Dickie and Doug at the funeral and we went out for dinner afterward and Dickie said, 'Do you know how much the Judge loved you?' It turns out the Judge told Dickie that he had this kid named Chris Nilan and he asked Dickie to go to [general manager] Sam Pollock and ask Sam to draft me for the Canadiens.

"In 1978 I got drafted in the 17th round by the Montreal Canadiens, No. 231 out of 235 total players drafted, and they only drafted me because the Judge went to Dickie Moore and Doug Harvey and went to bat for me. I had been a lifelong Bruins fan, but I was so happy to even get drafted by *any* team that I didn't mind too much that it was Montreal.

"But in 1978, when the Canadiens were going for their fourth straight Stanley Cup, I was rooting for the Bruins. I hadn't even been to Montreal yet, and the Canadiens may have had my rights, but the Bruins still had my heart. I was watching the game with my family, and when the Bruins took that too-many-men-on-the-ice penalty it broke my heart. But in the fall, I went off to training camp for the Canadiens, and it didn't take long for my allegiance to change."

When you're a 17th-round draft choice there are *no* expectations, and Nilan left training camp without a contract but with an opportunity to show what he could do.

"I remember at training camp they took a photo of me for the media guide with a Habs jersey on, and I couldn't believe it! This couldn't be happening! But the Canadiens sent me down and I had a five-game tryout, for $200.00 per game, with the Nova Scotia Voyageurs of the American Hockey League. I was happier than a pig in s—t! I was thinking, 'Man, I'm getting paid to play hockey!'"

So Nilan headed to Halifax, Nova Scotia, for the five-game tryout—and was not dressed for the first four games! You have five games to show you deserve a contract, and the coach doesn't even give you a chance until the fifth and final game of the tryout.

"The first four games were in Halifax, and I didn't even play in a single game, so my very first game was in Portland, Maine," Nilan said. "The previous season, the Maine Mariners had kicked the s—t out of the Nova Scotia Voyageurs and beat the V's four straight in the playoffs. The Mariners had a lot of tough guys on that team—[Frank] Bathe, [Mike] Busniuk, [Glen] Cochrane, [Jim] Cunningham—just a ton of very tough guys.

"My whole family came up to Portland—my mother and father, my brothers and sisters—and two shifts into the game I end up running Glen Cochrane. He was like Dave Brown's size. So he slashed me and I slashed him back, and we dropped our gloves and away we went. I hit him with a right and cut him open under his right eye. He went nuts, and I went crazy. He kept trying to come after me, and we both got kicked out of the game. My father was bulls—t with me! He said, 'We came all the way up here and you play two shifts!'

"But I got signed to a contract, and after I fought Glen every team we played against wanted to try me. It's not like I was going out after everybody! But everyone had heard what happened with Cochrane. I was playing physical, and I was playing tough, and the fights just came. One right after the other. The next thing

I knew I had 304 penalty minutes in 49 games! I was fighting every night!"

Nilan was immediately cast in a normal role for a hockey tough guy—protect the smaller, more skilled players and allow them to play their game.

"They put me on a line with Rick Meagher, who was a smaller, skilled center iceman," Nilan said. "I rode shotgun with him and played quite a bit. But I was also the beneficiary of *his* skills. I scored 15 goals and had 10 assists in those 49 games. All of a sudden people were thinking, 'Holy s—t! This guy can play a little bit too!'"

Nilan played those 49 games in the American Hockey League and fought almost every night. But it was the 50th game that haunted him—a 50th AHL game that never came.

"At one point Dave 'The Hammer' Schultz got sent down to Syracuse from Philadelphia and we were playing them on a Saturday night at the Metro Centre in Halifax," Nilan said. "He got sent down on Wednesday and I'm thinking, 'I can't wait! I'm gonna fight Dave Schultz on the weekend!' That would have been in my 50th game for Nova Scotia. But before we could play that game I got called up to Montreal, and believe it or not, I was actually a little bummed out because I thought, 'S—t! I'm gonna miss the chance to fight The Hammer!'"

The Montreal Canadiens were in need of some physical protection when they brought Nilan up. He would make his National Hockey League debut on February 26, 1980, against the Atlanta Flames.

"My first NHL game was against Atlanta, and I was a little bit scared," Nilan said. "They had a pretty big team, and I only played a couple of shifts a period. It felt like I had forgotten everything I had learned in the American League. I survived that first game and played the next couple of games. It was in my fourth game against the Philadelphia Flyers when I finally made my mark. I had my first NHL fight with Bob 'Battleship' Kelly, and I had an assist on the winning goal. That was it. I never went back and was fortunate enough to stay in the National Hockey League from that point on."

By that point in his young NHL career, Nilan already had a pretty good idea of what his role was and how he could stick with the Canadiens. He may have yearned to be a "hockey player" back in his days at Northeastern, but it became clear what Montreal needed from him.

"I stuck up for my teammates quite often," Nilan said. "There were a lot of times when I wasn't fighting for myself but fighting for the team. But there were also times when nothing necessarily happened to one of my guys on the ice, but I had to fight because I was challenged. There were a lot of times when I stepped in for guys and times when I kind of had to lead the charge, if you will.

"There were a number of times in those first 10 minutes of the game when I would answer the bell and kind of set the tone. I knew it gave my teammates a level of comfort in those situations. There were times when I might sense that a teammate was a little nervous about who we were playing, and I would go out early in the game and look for it. I would say, 'No time to be nervous, boys! I'm gonna start some s—t here and you better be ready to play, because it's coming! It's coming!'

I know my teammates were grateful for what I did. I know my centers certainly were. I played a lot on a line with Guy

Carbonneau and Bob Gainey, and I think they appreciated it. I certainly benefited from playing with those two guys. They allowed me to progress as a player to the point where I could play in almost any situation—except for killing penalties, because I was always in the box!"

Nilan was generally listed as 6'0", 205 pounds. That's a large man by normal societal standards, but for an NHL enforcer he was probably considered a bit undersized. Like others of similar stature, Chris made up for his relative lack of size with a fierce determination and a fearless approach to how he played the game, and especially with his willingness to fight. A common denominator for all the players in this book was playing the game with complete and total abandon.

Like everyone I've spoken to for this project, Nilan never acknowledges that any particular opponent gave him pause. He knew that a moment's hesitation could be the difference between winning and losing.

"No one gave me pause—and I don't say that like I'm some f—ing hero or tough guy," Nilan said. "But I couldn't afford to have that pause. A player of my ilk, if you show any pause to any of your teammates, they see it the same way. They see you go out there and drop your gloves and take charge. If you go out there and go after the biggest guy on the other team, they see that too.

"One of the questions that I hate is, 'Who was the toughest guy you ever fought?' I always say the same thing—I treated every one of those guys who did that job the exact same. I never felt like one guy was tougher than the next guy. I certainly knew if they fought right-handed or left-handed. I knew their tendencies.

Every one of those guys who did that job was tough as nails. And I respected them for that."

It was early on in Nilan's NHL career that he learned a difficult lesson: much of what he had picked up at the minor league level might not work at the NHL level against seriously tough opposition.

"We were playing the Bruins one night at the Forum, my first game against the Bruins, and I trucked Bobby Miller," Nilan said. "Stan Jonathan came right after me, and I fought Stan Jonathan. Next period, Doug Jarvis got kicked out of the face-off circle and Bob Gainey told me he would take the draw. I just told him I would do it, and I lined up against Terry O'Reilly. I beat O'Reilly on the draw, and he chopped me, so I chopped him back and we dropped the gloves. I *knew* he was a lefty. I hauled off and threw one punch. He came right back and hit me with two lefts right on the button. The blood poured out of my head, and I couldn't see. I didn't go down—I stayed on my feet.

"The linesman, John D'Amico, grabbed me and I had my head on his shoulder. As I lifted my head, I wiped the blood off on his shirt, and you wouldn't believe the s—t he said to me! I went to the penalty box, and Terry looked at me and pointed to his left hand.

"My pride was just destroyed that night! He put me in my place. Here was a guy I absolutely loved and adored as a player. I sat in that box and thought, 'I *cannot* fight like that and survive in this league.' Looking back on it, I'm so glad it happened that way, because I've seen guys lose fights early in their career and have their nose broken or their jaw broken, and their confidence is gone. At least only my pride was hurt."

For Nilan, that meant going back to school—fight school— and improving on what he did and how he did it. It also meant swallowing some pride and admitting that he didn't know what he didn't know. But he was willing to learn.

"I had to become a better technical fighter," Nilan said. "I had to learn when to open up and when to cover up. A guy like P.J. Stock—God love him!—was willing to take two or three good shots to land one big one. And he was always fighting guys bigger than him. But he also got hurt fighting that way. He took a huge shot and injured his eye, and it cut down on his career. I was certainly willing to trade shots, but I also had to be smart about it."

Nilan certainly had his battles against his hometown Boston Bruins. But one of the most famous, involving Terry O'Reilly, began with a couple of cheap shots directed at Nilan by a goaltender, of all players.

"The famous story between me and the Bruins actually started with [goaltender] Pete Peeters," Nilan said. "He stuck me in the balls a couple of times, and I finally said, 'Listen, you do that again and I'm gonna take your f—ing head off!' And I think Terry O'Reilly actually went to Pete and told him to just let me alone—don't wake me up. So Pete did it again, and the play went up to the other end of the ice, but I just turned around. It was like the Bruins had a power play up at the other end.

"I came back and cross-checked Peeters in the mask, and he went down. So O'Reilly came the length of the rink to get after me. I had my back to the wall, and I know he's coming, so I'm just getting ready. And that's when I hit him. I'm gonna tell ya, that might be the hardest punch I ever threw and connected with in a game. He went down right away, and I cut him up pretty bad. When he went down, I didn't hit him again though. I couldn't hold my stick in my hand for like two weeks after that, but I fought two nights later in Philadelphia against Dave Brown!

"I think Terry was really pissed off at Pete Peeters. He said something in the newspaper the next day. He said, 'I told him to leave that guy alone, and don't wake him up!' There were certainly nights going into the Boston Garden where it was nerve wracking! But you can't show it. Those Bruins teams had [Wayne] Cashman, [Al] Secord, O'Reilly, [John] Wensink, Jonathan—I mean, come on! That was an uneasy feeling. And the same sort of feeling going into Philadelphia. But you've got to be able to stand up to it and walk through that fear."

Of course, the other famous Nilan–Bruins incident involved a decidedly nonconfrontational player in skilled Bruins forward Rick Middleton. There is disagreement to this very day about exactly what happened. And as other hockey tough guys have said, it was something Nilan would like to have back.

"We were fighting for the puck in the corner, and I *never* went after guys like Rick Middleton. I just didn't," Nilan said. "That wasn't my M.O. Rick came up and clipped me with the stick in the head, and [referee] Kerry Fraser didn't call anything. And look, a lot of times s—t happens to tough guys and they just let it go. And I was pissed off after Rick clipped me, and Frasier didn't call anything. Of course, Kerry has his version of what happened, and I have mine.

"If I had just taken my top hand off of my stick and gave him a backhander, it would have been the same result. I *did not* hit him with the butt end of my stick! I hit him with the outside of my top hand, my left hand, in the jaw. It was with my glove! If I had my stick outside of my glove, I would have ripped his face open. I hit him with the back of my glove, but I jolted him good. He had false teeth and they went through his lip and cut him open. I don't believe I knocked any of his permanent teeth out. It certainly looked like a butt end, but I will go to my grave saying I hit him with my glove! If I butt-ended him, I would have owned up. I'm not a f—ing liar! That's one thing I'm not.

"I will say this—for me, it was the most regrettable thing I ever did in my 13 seasons. It's something I regret, and I've apologized to Ricky. I've spent time with him since then and it's long been put to bed. But I truly regret that I did it. It's something that I wish I never did."

Perhaps the most infamous night of Nilan's career took place on May 14, 1987, when the Canadiens and Flyers had an epic 40-minute total team brawl—*before* the game! Nilan spent the entire time fighting with legendary Flyers enforcer Dave Brown, not once but twice. It was before the series-deciding seventh game and Nilan admitted he had nothing left in the game, which the Flyers won by a goal to advance to the Stanley Cup Final. But, reminiscent of the Roman gladiators, Nilan and Brown knew full well *they* had to fight, and they did. Ironically, neither was involved with instigating the brawl, and both were in their respective dressing rooms when it began, but neither hesitated about what their roles meant to the team. You can only imagine the physical toll a nearly 40-minute fight with Dave Brown would do to anyone. And Nilan was five inches shorter and 15 pounds lighter than Brown.

The other famous fight Nilan was involved in took place on April 20, 1984, between the Montreal Canadiens and Quebec Nordiques—the Good Friday Massacre. I have to admit I had forgotten about this particular night until John Shannon reminded me about it. And remember—Shannon said he felt the Good Friday Massacre was much more violent than the Stanley Cup pregame brawl in 1987.

Looking back on it, Nilan admitted there had been building tensions between the two Quebec-based NHL franchises.

"Look, it was never going to be what the Bruins–Canadiens rivalry was, and it could never reach that level," Nilan said. "But the Nordiques had been improving on the ice, and the tensions built between the two teams over the years."

Nilan even agrees with Shannon that this game was more violent than the playoff brawl, and he says it all goes back to something that happened at the end of the second period.

"The two teams had kind of gathered together, and Louis Sleigher was standing next to Jean Hamel," Nilan said. "Now, those two guys had been roommates when they both played for Quebec, but for some reason, Sleigher sucker-punched Jean right in the eye and knocked him out. Mario Tremblay had been trying to act like the peacemaker, but he ended up smashing Peter Stastny in the nose, and it was on."

There had already been four fighting majors, four roughing minors, three slashing penalties, an elbow, and a slash before the brawl actually broke out, so you've got a pretty good idea of how physical and mean the game was. Those were among the reasons both Nilan and Shannon called it a violent game.

The referee, Bruce Hood, sent both teams to their respective dressing rooms while he and the linesmen tried to sort out the penalties. When the two teams returned to the ice and were warming up before the third period, the public address announcer started telling the crowd—and the players—what had been assessed. What the players didn't yet realize was that 11 of them had been given game misconducts and thrown out of the game.

"Bruce Hood, God rest his soul, was the referee and he had a thing about me," Nilan said. "He and I never seemed to get along during my career. He gave me a double fighting major, a 10-minute misconduct, and a game misconduct. Now, I *had* taken a punch at Randy Moller, and deserved a fighting major for the one, but I have no idea where Bruce got the second fighting major."

Larry Robinson said at the time that as players learned they had already been thrown out of the game, they felt they had nothing to lose, so both teams started brawling. And Nilan admits that the Canadiens had a particular target in mind.

"We really wanted to get at Louis Sleigher because of what he had done to Jean," Nilan said. 'We didn't know it at the time, but Jean was out until training camp the next season with that eye injury. Then he got hurt in an exhibition game and was never able to play again. Jean Hamel might have been the nicest guy I've ever played with, and he still doesn't come around to Canadiens alumni events. I really miss seeing him."

Among the "highlights" of that second brawl between the two was a fight between Dale Hunter (Nordiques) and his brother, Mark (Canadiens).

"I'm not sure how much Mark really wanted to fight with his brother, but he was sticking up for a teammate, and we all appreciated that," Nilan said.

When the third period finally began, the Nordiques held onto a slim 1–0 lead, and they were trailing in the series three games to two, facing elimination. Chris remembers that a single player was not going to give the Nordiques new life.

"Michel Goulet gave Quebec a 2–0 lead early in the third period, and then Steve Shutt just took over. He scored two goals to tie the game, and we scored five in a row, eventually winning the game 5–3 and clinching the series. Steve just wouldn't let us lose that game."

By the way, Bruce Hood, who was roundly criticized for his handling of the brawls, retired at the end of the Stanley Cup playoffs. Whether that was at the NHL's request or not was never revealed.

In January 1988, Nilan was traded to the New York Rangers, where he spent the next two and a half seasons. Then, in June of 1990, it finally happened. Nilan was acquired by the team he had grown up idolizing, the Boston Bruins.

"The first time I went into the Bruins' locker room up at their practice rink in Wilmington, I'm sitting in the room getting ready," Nilan said. "Gordie Kluzak came in and starts yelling to the trainer, 'I can't believe this! He's here and he's a Bruin—and you're gonna sit him right next to me!' But he was fine.

"My first game as a Bruin, I was nervous as hell. I wondered what the fans would think about me because of my experiences *against* that team! Ray [Bourque] said to me, 'Knucks! What's wrong with you? Bruins fans are going to accept you!' And they did. It was a good feeling coming home and being accepted by the fan base that had been chanting 'NILAN SUCKS!' on so many evenings.

"I had fallen in love with hockey because of Bobby Orr and the Big, Bad Bruins, and now I was wearing that Spoked B. My first year with Mike Milbury as coach was great. Then I broke my ankle, which was f—ing stupid! I was playing basketball out in the Garden on the Celtics floor and broke my ankle! I think Mike kind of soured on me after that. I *loved* playing for Mike Milbury! I would go through a wall for him!"

Milbury was roundly criticized for selecting a couple of players considered less than All-Star caliber—particularly Nilan and checker Brian Skrudland—ahead of stars like Kirk Muller and Guy Lafleur. It was an acknowledgment by Milbury of the importance of the role player to a team, and to this day he says he has no regrets for selecting those players. Unfortunately, both Nilan and Skrudland were injured and unable to play in the All-Star game.

The following season, Milbury moved into the Bruins' front office and hired Rick Bowness as the new head coach. From Nilan's perspective, the change behind the Boston bench was night and day.

"My last year there I got a little pissed off," Nilan said. "The Bruins had the A and B squads in training camp, and if you're on the B squad, you're either heading up to Portland, Maine, or you're heading out the door. They put me on the B squad, and I was wondering why they were doing that to me at that stage of my career. I knew I wasn't Ray Bourque or Cam Neely, but I had been in the league as long as they had! I thought I had earned a little bit of respect.

"Rick Bowness was the coach that year, and it just didn't start well. They had Alan Stewart and L.B. (Lyndon Byers) there, and it was obvious those guys were going to get the ice time. The Bruins went on that annual long road trip to start the season, and I didn't play one game on that five-game trip. I remember we were in Chicago Stadium the last game of the trip and I was dressed for warm-up, so I thought I was finally going to get to play. 'No,' Bowness said. 'Take your stuff off.'

"So I got on the bike and I started pedaling, and Bowness walked by and said, 'I'm really proud of how you're handling this.' And I answered, 'Handling what? Being treated like a piece of s—t!'

"No one even spoke to me, and I think I had earned more respect than they were showing me.

"L.B. and Stewart both fought in that Chicago game, and we finished the game and went back to Boston. Stewart packed up his car and quit hockey the very next day, and L.B. broke his ankle. All of a sudden, Bowness comes to me after the morning skate and sits next to me like I'm his best friend. He says, 'Hey, I hope you're ready to go tonight. Are you ready to go?' I just told Rick to go f—k himself. So I didn't play—that game or any of the others that followed."

It was clear to everyone that Nilan and Rick Bowness were just not going to get along. The animosity between the two was obvious even to members of the press. The venerable Joe Fitzgerald of the *Boston Herald* finally wrote about it in the newspaper.

"After Joe Fitz wrote about the situation in the *Boston Herald*, I had a meeting with Mike Milbury and Rick Bowness. Mike told me I couldn't talk to the coach like that, and I just said, 'Well, I did! And here's why! I felt like I was being disrespected. I wasn't asking anyone to kiss my ass, but I was just looking for a little respect.'

"It was totally different with Mike as the coach the season before. I would do anything he asked me to do! There was a respect factor there. Don't misunderstand me—I actually think Rick Bowness is a really good guy, and I think Harry [Sinden] and Mike were pushing all the buttons. I just had to stand up for myself. I always put the team ahead of myself, but this one time I felt I had to stand my ground and be true to myself. And I did. It eventually cost me."

As always happens to NHL tough guys, there was the inevitable realization that the job was getting too tough—physically and mentally.

"I was near the end of my career at that point, and it was getting tougher and tougher on me to do what I did," Nilan said. "It was certainly getting tougher mentally. I was going through the things that older guys went through when I was coming up. Young guys wanted to try me because I had a certain reputation as a fighter. I fought Jim McKenzie and Stu Grimson in back-to-back games. I hung in there with them, and I was certainly willing to fight them, but it was getting more and more difficult.

"If I was honest with myself, I was coming to the end of my career. On the inside, I knew that, but on the outside, I couldn't let anyone know that I was near the end. I kept showing up, I kept fighting. I did the best I could at that time. Like a lot of guys, it wasn't easy coming to grips with that. It was hard to be brutally honest with yourself."

The Bruins placed Nilan on waivers in February 1992, and the Montreal Canadiens gave him a chance to go back to the team he had begun his career with. But the return was bittersweet.

"I ended up playing for Montreal at the end of the season, but the writing was on the wall," Nilan said. "I wanted to play one more year after that, but Jacques Demers came in and he wanted Rob Ramage and they didn't want two older guys on the team. Demers wanted Ramage over me. So that was it. I could have chased another year—gone to L.A. or some other place—but I had come full circle. I was able to retire with the team I had started with, and I walked away."

Chris had 222 fights in the National Hockey League and certainly won more than he lost. But there is no way anyone can be in 222 bare-knuckle battles and not have it take a toll. Believe it or not, it's not something that he dwells on.

"No, I don't really think of that very much," Nilan said. "If there is something that I feel, it's probably in my hands a little bit. Look, my body is beat up and I feel it. I've had knee replacements, I've got screws in my ankle, I've had a bunch of surgeries. But as far as the mental toll? I don't think so. Like I said, one thing I'm not is a f—ing liar!

"I had one time when I believe I had a concussion, even though I didn't have those symptoms the next day. I tried to cut in on Fred Barrett in Minnesota one time, and he hit me with his shoulder right in the jaw. I was in la-la land! I was going to go after him, and Mario Tremblay was yelling at me, 'NO! NO!' I came back to the bench and my head was spinning.

"The next day I was fine, though.

"I never got hit in a fight with a punch that did anything like that to me. Now, did I have a few lumps on my head, here and there? Yeah, of course. A couple of cuts? Yeah. I never broke my nose or my jaw or anything like that. Even if I did have documented concussions, it's not something I would worry about. You can't spend your life worrying about that s—t.

"I would be much more worried about things being passed down from my family. My mother is having dementia right now. Is that hereditary, or is that something with how she lived her life? I don't know. I would be more worried about something like that than something from how I made my living.

"Some people may think that's stupid, but I'm not gonna waste my life worrying about something from my past that I can't change anyway. Now, if there was a test that I could take to see how my brain was right now, would I be willing to do that? Sure, I would. But until there is I'm not gonna sit here and worry about it. I read a lot and keep my mind active that way."

Nilan has always been honest about his own off-ice battles with drugs and alcohol. He has been brutally honest even when talking to school kids about his heroin addiction. But Nilan, as always, battled through and overcame the odds.

When you're in recovery, there are not a lot of opportunities out there. But one of those chances came from Mitch Melnick, host of the *Melnick in the Afternoon* program in Montreal. Nilan appeared on the program often, and it led to Melnick setting up a meeting for him with station management. Nilan agreed to move from Oregon, where he was living with his girlfriend Jamie Holtz, for a full-time position with the station.

Nilan worked for the station until 2022, when the parent company, Bell Media, required all employees to get vaccinated for Covid-19. Those who refused would be summarily fired.

"First of all, I'm staying true to myself. I've done quite a bit of research and I've also looked at my own health issues. I applied for a medical exemption from getting the Covid vaccine and Bell Media told me they didn't respect my decision to not get vaccinated. They told me they were going to fire me if I didn't get the vaccine.

"I don't disrespect anyone who decided to get vaccinated and wanted to do it. I don't agree with people who think I'm being selfish because I didn't get vaccinated. There is almost no one who got vaccinated for someone else. They may claim they did it for their mother or their grandmother, but they got vaccinated, for the most part, because they were afraid of getting Covid.

"I survived Covid. I had it at the beginning, which would give me natural immunity, and that should be better than a vaccine. I'm willing to accept the consequences, although it's not easy. I didn't disrespect anyone else's decision, for whatever reasons they might have. I was almost ready to get vaccinated to keep my job, and my girlfriend, Jamie, told me, 'Hold on for a second. We had Covid. Let's look at this closer.' We discussed it. I did not get vaccinated and accepted the consequences."

With all that he has overcome in his life, you might think Chris Nilan would be bitter. You would be wrong. Despite everything, Nilan maintains as positive an outlook as anyone could possibly hope for.

"My father died, and I lost my best friend, Larry Jackson," Nilan said. "I lost my job, and my sister, Susan, has cancer. Bodie, my dog, recently passed away from lymphoma. Bodie changed my life getting sober and helped me with so many issues. He was the best friend I've ever had. I've had a lot of bad s—t happen that before I would have drank or drugged my way through to not feel it. Life is certainly difficult, but I've never been happier in my life! Life is good."

CHAPTER 8

JAY MILLER

———

I'M SITTING ON THE PATIO behind the sprawling clubhouse of the Sacconnesset Golf Club in Falmouth, Massachusetts. Directly below me is a bird's-eye view of the 18th green, and to my right is a pond with a dory tied up in the middle of it, as part of the first tee. Former Boston Bruins and Los Angeles Kings forward Jay Miller suggested we meet here for lunch to renew our acquaintance and talk about his National Hockey League career. He's already called and told me he was running late but to grab a table and order whatever I want for lunch.

Miller limps in about 15 minutes later (he is three months removed from a left knee replacement), and it's obvious that he is a regular. Mary, our server, greets him like an old friend and, without being asked, sets a can of Coke in front of him. They tell me they've known each other for more than 30 years, and there is an obvious affection between the two. It isn't until 30 minutes have passed that I learn Miller isn't just a regular—he's a minority owner of Sacconnesset. It's only a small part of Miller's impressive post-playing career empire.

Jay and his wife, Paula (née Pirini), are the owners of the Courtyard Restaurant and Pub in Cataumet. Trust me, the list of successful restaurants owned by former professional athletes is unfortunately short. But the Courtyard has been going for 25 years. (The pan-seared scallops with spinach risotto are superb!) In a lot of ways, Miller's restaurant success stems from principles established in his successful NHL career—work hard, never give up, do the job, move on.

Miller was a fourth-round draft choice (66th overall) of the Quebec Nordiques in the 1980 NHL Entry Draft. But the Nordiques were upset that Miller was unwilling to sign and turn professional and quickly soured on his major league capabilities. He had just finished his freshman year playing for Charlie Holt at the University of New Hampshire, and he wanted to get his college education. In fact, he played at UNH for four seasons and was able to get a three-game stint with the Fredericton Express of the American Hockey League at the end of his college career.

But for Miller, it felt like the writing was on the wall.

"Quebec let me go, and I was kind of kicking around a couple of minor league teams, just trying to catch on. I fought a couple of times, but I really didn't do very well. It just wasn't my bag. I just didn't get mad enough. I figured I was already at the end of my hockey career, and I was ready to fall back on my business degree. I wasn't making very much money, and I didn't think I was very good."

It was the advice of one of those minor league coaches that likely changed the course of Miller's career—and perhaps his life.

"I was playing for the Mohawk Stars, and [coach] Rick Ley said to me, 'Jay, I just saw you beat up one of the toughest guys down here. You completely pummeled him without even breathing hard, and then went out and scored a goal. Have you ever thought about dropping your gloves more often?'

"He went on to say, 'If you want to make it to the NHL, you have most of the skills. You're not fast enough, but boy can you f—ing fight!'

"I said, 'Fight? I'm a kid from Natick who doesn't know anything about fighting.' I grew up watching players like Stan Jonathan, John Wensink, Dave Schultz, and guys like that, but I certainly never thought of myself in that way. So I started going to the boards hard and going to the front of the net and these guys started dropping their gloves. I wasn't looking for it, but it just started.

"I'll never forget talking to a guy named Jock Callander, who played for the Pittsburgh Penguins. He said, 'Jay, you're beating up guys who want to be in the NHL, and all they've done is fight from their junior days right on up. You're making them look like four-year-olds!'"

As his teammates and opponents observed, Miller may not have had much fighting experience, but he seemed to be adept at it. Teammates loved it for the obvious reason—Miller protected them and gave them room to play their game in relative safety. But it also turned out that the team's owner had a vested interest in seeing Miller continue with his newfound pugilistic prowess.

Anyone who made the cut for this book had a certain penchant for fighting. But watch a few videos of Jay Miller's fights, and there is a ferociousness that seems to be missing from the others. Some NHL tough guys seem almost clinical with how they approach the fight game. For a guy who says he just didn't get mad enough to fight early on, Miller seems to come *unhinged* at times when he battles. Miller had a career-high 33 fights in the 1987–88 season and a total of 164 fights over his seven-year, 446-game career.

"Rick Ley kept harping on it, and the owner of the team, Victor Ehre, came to me and said, 'Everyone loves how you're playing the game. I'll give you $200 for every fight you have.' He brought me along to Muskegon the next season, and then I started *really* fighting.

"But I didn't feel like I was going anywhere, so I was getting ready to quit hockey and use my business degree. I was selling and building swimming pools in the offseason and making decent money at it. I was making $60,000 a year digging pools in the summer. I actually sold Charlie Simmer his first pool."

Miller returned to Massachusetts ready to dig those pools and work toward a career away from the game. That was until he got a call from his agent, Joe Lyons, who told Miller he had arranged a tryout with the Boston Bruins. How could a kid from Natick turn that opportunity down? He couldn't. But it also didn't take him long to make an impression.

"We're playing shinny hockey two days before training camp at Hockeytown in Danvers," Miller said. "We're not even wearing shoulder pads or elbow pads. I'm in a locker room that only the scrubs are in—the Bruins are in another locker room entirely. There are no refs, we just go out on the ice and play shinny.

"I run the Bruins' No. 1 draft pick, Gordie Kluzak (6'6", 225 pounds), and I didn't even know he was their No. 1 pick.

We're playing shinny, and I run the first overall pick in the draft right over. Ray Bourque is sitting on the bench next to the team's resident tough guy, John Blum, and Blum tells Ray, 'I'll take care of this kid right now!' We drop the gloves and three punches later Johnny Blum is down on the ice.

"I go back to the opposing team's bench and Ray says to his teammates, 'I thought someone was going to take care of this!' Brian Curran looks at Ray and tells him, 'I got this guy!' Curran comes out and drops the gloves and yells at me, 'You can't treat my players like this! You're not a Bruin!' Five punches and Curran is down on the ice, and now everyone is jumping me, trying to help Curran. Ray, on the bench, says, 'I guess no one is going to take care of him, huh?'

"I got signed by the Bruins three hours later. I didn't know it, but Harry Sinden was sitting in the stands, and I guess he saw enough."

Miller began the season playing in the American Hockey League for Moncton. But he was not destined to spend a lot of time in the Maritimes.

"I'm playing in the minors for the Moncton Golden Flames," Miller said. "I had 113 penalty minutes in 18 games, so I guess I got some attention and the Bruins called me up. On November 23, 1985, I'm making my NHL debut at the Garden against the Philadelphia Flyers and they've got Dave Brown. I knew Brown a little bit from playing against him in the minors, and I knew how big and strong he was. But I'm in the Garden, and all of my family and friends are there watching me, and it's just time to go. I knew he was a lefty, and didn't fight as well right-handed, and I guess that's why I got him so good. But we fought a few more times than that." In fact, Jay Miller and Dave Brown fought a total of nine times over the course of their NHL careers.

By the way, if you want to surprise Miller and most every NHL enforcer, ask them who they fought with most during their career. They almost never get it right, and when I informed Miller his most regular opponent was Gord Donnelly, I got an immediate and emphatic response.

"Get the f—k out of here! Really? I thought I fought Bob Probert more than anybody. No s—t! And Donnelly was afraid of me. You shock me!"

That began a three-plus-year stint for Miller playing for his hometown Boston Bruins. Now if you know anything about Boston fans, you know they love and appreciate their tough guys, and Miller became a bit of a folk hero. In the 1987–88 season he racked up 304 penalty minutes in 78 games, breaking the team record that was held by the man who was standing behind the Bruins bench as coach, the venerable Terry O'Reilly.

"I hated Taz as a coach because he pushed me *so* hard, but I also loved him," Miller said. "An old coach once told me, 'If your coach isn't pushing you, he doesn't like you! So get over it!' Taz was a different breed. I could never, ever be Terry O'Reilly. I was never that person. I never got mad enough. In the few fights when I did get mad, you see me go absolutely bananas!"

Every player I've talked to for this book has had a moment he would like to change. That 1987–88 season also led to the one moment in Miller's career that he would like to have back. It came in the Stanley Cup Final against the Edmonton Oilers. The game was on May 20, 1988, at the Boston Garden and the Oilers had a 1–0 lead in the final.

"If I could take back one thing in my career it was in 1988, taking that penalty," Miller said. "It was the playoff game against Edmonton when the lights went out at the Boston Garden. Michael Thelven got run over, I think by Kevin McClelland. Terry was so mad, he wanted to get blood, and he tapped me on the shoulder. The press didn't know it, and a lot of the players didn't know it. Wayne Gretzky said he knew Terry was going to send me out, and he told McClelland to just fold up and let me punch him. I don't have many, if any, regrets in my career, but that's one I would probably like to take back."

The game was tied 2–2 when Jay went after McClelland. Both got roughing minors and 10-minute misconducts, and they had fought each other in the first period. But the Oilers seemed to gain momentum from the altercation, and Gretzky scored just 24 seconds later to give the Oilers the lead. An empty-net goal from Jari Kurri sealed the deal, giving Edmonton the 4–2 win and two victories in Boston to start the series. They would go on to win the Cup.

Miller's 17 penalty minutes don't seem that excessive and pale in comparison to the 32 minutes he had against Buffalo earlier in the playoffs, but it was the momentum swing, and the Edmonton win, that still grates on Miller all these years later.

Unlike some legendary NHL tough guys, Miller claims he rarely, if ever, was out of control on the ice. He is very laid-back away from the rink and even approached fighting against heavyweights the same way.

"I never fought mad, but fear was my biggest asset...fear of losing the respect of the players in my dressing room," Miller said. "I had 18 guys on my bench who relied on me. I did not want to lose, personally, which would hurt my team. That was my biggest fear and my biggest asset. That was my job—sit at the end of the bench and growl.

"I don't think in my whole career I ever cheap-shotted one person," Miller said. "With all the majors I had, I don't think I ever did that—well, maybe Ulf Samuelsson. Most of the guys I fought were bigger than me, taller than me. I wanted to get in tight because I knew my asset was in that position. Joey Kocur wanted to stretch you out and throw one big punch, but that could be dangerous for me. Simple physics tell me that taking a punch from in close was a lot better than taking a punch from five feet away. Some guys played with a switch, but my switch was five punches. I had to take three to five to get my s—t together and I was willing to take those three to five.

"Listen, every fight hurts, and don't let anyone tell you different, but I was most proud that I never hurt *my* team when I fought. I might have tied once in a while, Scott Stevens may have got me a few times, Rick Tocchet—maybe some of the guys I wasn't ready for. John Kordic hit me a couple of times once, and I swear to God the lights went out. Chris Nilan wasn't big enough, he didn't have the brawn to seriously hurt me, but when Kordic hit you, it hurt.

"I was also proud that I didn't take the misconducts and do stupid stuff. I didn't act like I was wearing the belt after a fight, or flip the fans off—well, maybe one time. I didn't want to do anything that would motivate the other team. My fight was meant to motivate my team and demoralize the other team. Stamina was also one of my biggest assets."

While Miller and I were sitting on that deck at Sacconnessett, he got a phone call from his wife, Paula. He put her on speaker, told her what we were doing, and asked her if he ever lost a fight in the National Hockey League. The answer was immediate—and definitive.

"The only player my husband ever lost to? Rick Tocchet," Paula said. "Rick was like a Rock 'Em, Sock 'Em Robot, and I told Rick years later that he was the only player I ever saw beat my husband up! There were bigger guys that Jay fought—gosh, Dave Brown was a giant!—and I just remember Jay punching up against Brown!"

Miller can be very self-deprecating. He certainly is not a braggart, but don't mistake that for not being a proud professional athlete who was *very* dedicated to his craft and felt he was pretty good at it.

"It pisses me off when guys in the press don't think I'm one of the top fighters in the NHL," Miller said. "In my own mind, I feel like I was in the top five. I never gave up, I never got misconducts, I was always clean and fair. I did it the correct way, and I always knew what I was doing. I'm not bragging when I say that, but I know I did what I was supposed to do. I was sitting on the plane later in my career talking with Luc Robitaille and Wayne Gretzky and Luc said, 'Jay, you're the only guy who can't take a night off. We can go for a two-game skid and not score a point, but you take one night off and we're screwed!'

"Ten years after I finished playing, a bunch of us were sitting around my bar having a pop or two, and Geoff Courtnall told me that guys used to puke before the games thinking about who was going to have to fight Jay Miller. I called my wife and said, 'You won't believe what these guys are saying about me!' See, when you're playing you don't know any of that. To this day, I don't think of myself as a star fighter or in any other way.

"I'm proud to be thought of as one of the toughest players in Bruins history. I know I'm not No. 1, but I certainly think I'm right there at two or three. I think the guys that I played with would tell you that. I'm hurt that many around the NHL don't consider me to be the "real deal." I didn't overexpose myself like some guys do. I wasn't flamboyant or talked about myself very much.

"I didn't believe in undressing in front of the public. I had my sweaters custom fit in the arms and around the neck. I had triple tie-downs around the side. Because once you can't see, it's no good! I never pulled sweaters over guys' heads. I never took a second shot at a guy when they were down. I didn't believe in that. Okay, I might have done a couple just because they were assholes! I tried to hurt them, but I didn't want to take advantage of guys."

Miller and the Bruins moved on to the 1988–89 season and beginning with the Thanksgiving holiday, the team started to go into a slide. They won just twice in a 16-game stretch and Bruins fans were growing restless.

"I knew someone was going to get traded, but when Tom Johnson called me in my hotel room, I was so devastated," Miller said. "I had given my heart and soul to the Bruins and maybe it could be justified if I got cut and picked up by someone else, but I never, ever deserved to be traded.

"It's the business and I get that, but trust me, I learned it was *the* best thing that ever happened to me in my life. I was going to make $125,000 playing for the Bruins, and the Kings gave me $1.3 million over three years. Other tough guys were going to their GMs after I got signed and looking for more money from their teams too!"

But if you ask Miller, even today, why he was traded to the Los Angeles Kings, he says it was for one simple reason.

"I think the Bruins felt like they had to make a move," Miller said. "I don't think they wanted to, and it was like a lot of trades that teams don't necessarily want to make. But Gretz insisted on it, and he kind of ran the league at that point. He wanted protection, and he knew I was loyal off the ice too.

"I ended up going from Boston to Los Angeles for one big reason—Gretz wanted me. I was told 20 years after I got traded that there were Bruins fans wearing black armbands because I was gone. Harry Sinden and I are friends, and I thank him every time I see him for trading me to the Kings. I tripled my salary and I got to play with one of the best players who ever played."

Miller had developed a reputation while serving as an enforcer for the Bruins. But he came to feel that Gretzky needed him more off the ice than on it.

"I honestly believe that my teammates trusted me off the ice too," Miller said. "Gretz wanted somebody he could trust and help protect him from the s—theads who are out there, off the ice. He was a team player, but when he was away from the game he wanted to be left alone and just relax. When I came to Los Angeles, Marty McSorley said to me, 'You're up!' I didn't understand what he meant at the time, but he meant I was up watching after the big boy. And Wayne needed it.

"I think he appreciated what I did, as a friend.

"I didn't really have to protect Wayne on the ice. I just had to make sure I was ready to do something to help change the game when it was called for. Wayne was to hockey what Tiger Woods was to golf. He did *not* need protection on the ice. A rising tide lifts all boats. There were only like three guys who were tasked to "protect" him on the ice—Dave Semenko, Marty McSorley, and me. Wayne was a player of Bobby Orr status, Michael Jordan status, Tiger Woods status."

Like every tough guy I've ever spoken to, Miller adheres to what is commonly called the Code. Everyone has their own idea of what that entails, but the overall components are fairly universal. And not every tough guy believes in every part of the Code.

"Part of the Code is that you don't do to someone else what you wouldn't want done to you, but I disagree with that in one respect," Miller said. "I didn't care what they did to me, I knew I would get them back, if at all possible, down the road. I never held a grudge, but I remembered!

"Dave Brown and Bob Probert were two guys I had a check-mark against in the book, not because they did anything wrong, but because I knew they were the biggest and baddest guys in the league and I wanted to make sure I was there with them. That was my motivation, in addition to my guys watching from the bench. Nilan, Kordic—pfft! If it happens, it happens.

"Chris was a smart fighter. He never wanted to give up until he was out cold. He was going to keep going, which I respected. I was the same way. You take five shots and I'm going to keep going. But if you did something stupid—knee me, bite me—that was a checkmark, and I *will* get you back.

"Was there ever a sleepless night or sleepless pregame nap? Are you f—ing kidding me? Every time! I told you, guys like me never get a night off! You don't want to lose. It doesn't matter if I beat this guy up the last time, the minute the game is over, I'm thinking about the next game and the next tough guy.

"Now when I went out with the guys after the game—Gretz, Ray, or any of my teammates—it was over. It was completely over. The next morning, I would read the stats and ask guys about someone they might have played with or against. And you get yourself ready for the next game."

And if you want to get Miller fired up—even on the porch at Sacconnessett—try asking him if he worries about the toll playing the enforcer's role might have had on him, years later.

"We got paid to do something we loved! Anyone who complains about the *toll* taken or sues the NHL—give me a break! You picked that career. You weren't worried about concussions or CTE when you were taking those paychecks. I probably had 10 concussions! My wife thinks I had 30 of them! Who knows? But we got paid to do a job, and we knew the risks when we took it on. At the time of the first shift of a game, I was apprehensive because I was afraid of losing. But once we got going, I loved it and couldn't wait to do it again. I couldn't wait to hear, 'Miller! You're up!' I think I was the highest-paid per-shift player in league history!

"Overall, I feel pretty good for 62 years old. My hands are pretty bad and my shoulders a little bit. I just had a knee replaced. But I took care of myself. I worked out hard! I used to take a bike from Falmouth to Framingham and back for fun! I power-lifted for strength, overall strength. I needed stamina, leg power, and shoulder power."

Miller has seen fighting diminish in hockey over the years, and he seems ambivalent about it. If the people who run the sport want fighting out of the game, Miller has no problem with that. But he also points out that if fighting is ever eliminated from the game completely, it will never come back. He points out that it would be politically incorrect to bring fighting back after deeming it too dangerous to the participants now. When it's gone, it will be gone.

For every player—even Tom Brady—there comes a time to end a career. For Miller, it happened in the preseason before the 1992–93 season.

"I was in the hallway with Chris Nilan, who I had never met," Miller said. "We were doing sticks together. It was an exhibition game, and we knew we were going to fight that night. People wanted to see it. He didn't mind, and I didn't mind. We weren't going to kill each other. Rogie Vachon, our GM, and their GM had seen us talking in the hallway.

"We got to the airport later and I was told that [Kings coach] Barry Melrose didn't think he needed me anymore. If I wanted to go to Boston, no problem. If I wanted to go to Winnipeg, I could go. They said I wasn't going to double-dip, and if the other team didn't want to pay me, so be it. I just said, 'Then I'm not going.' I took the sweater off my back. Maybe I could have played a couple more years, but I knew the kids were tougher and I had my time. I had seen a lot of tough guys before me try to hang on, and I didn't want to be that. I saw legitimate tough guys who were just horrible at the end. I knew right then I had to go make a career somewhere else."

Miller has even had opportunities to work in the NHL after hanging up his skates. He could certainly help young players learn how to protect themselves, even when the game has turned from the one he grew up in. He was never tempted.

"I had a chance to, but the last thing I wanted to do was work in the NHL when I was done. I had always picked the brains of business leaders and learned from them. Those were the people who were going to lead me into the second stage of my life.

"Hockey gave me a living, but it was a steppingstone to where I wanted to go. And I've been very fortunate. I don't wake up in the morning worrying about my money. I have real estate all over the Cape, and varying business interests."

Miller is still a popular figure among his former teammates. He still hears from some of the best players who ever played—people like Wayne Gretzky, Luv Robitaille, Cam Neely, and Ray Bourque. He is gruff and direct but fiercely loyal, and if you're his friend you likely will be for life. Even tough guys can get philosophical at times, and Miller remembers fondly a day near the end of his time with the Boston Bruins.

"Ray Bourque, Cam Neely, and I sat next to each other in the locker room, and I remember saying to them one time, 'Do you realize how fortunate we are? Monetarily, family-wise, and where we are, how lucky we are?'

"But post-career, fear was again my biggest asset. I just didn't want to lose. I don't fall in love with my projects, I have a wife who is not only my best friend but an amazing businesswoman. But did I ever expect what I have today? Not really. I would have just been happy to get a good job, but I never envisioned what I have today. I've never had a boss. If things ended tomorrow, I could honestly say I've had a wonderful life."

CHAPTER 9

MIKE MILBURY

———————

DADS HAVE PHRASES that drive their kids nuts. One of my favorites is, "Don't ask the question if you don't want to hear the answer!" Oh, my kids *love* that one. The same can be said of Mike Milbury. The former NHL defenseman, coach, general manager, and broadcaster is never afraid to tell you exactly what he thinks about almost any topic. So of course I had to talk to him for this project. But first I had to answer some questions for him.

"What is this project? And why do you want to talk to me?"

I explained that the book is about legendary hockey tough guys and some of the stories they have to share.

"Who have you talked to?"

I ran through a partial list—Archie Henderson, Dave Brown, Jay Miller, Chris Nilan.

"Well, I fought Archie Henderson—not very well!—fought Chris Nilan, fought Dave Brown. I may have been involved with many of the guys in this book. Let's go!"

And that's what we did for more than an hour.

It started with Milbury's recollection about his first encounter with Dave Brown of the Philadelphia Flyers and Brown's first NHL game against the Boston Bruins.

"I was getting ready for an afternoon game against the Flyers, and the guard at the dressing room door at the old Boston Garden told me, 'There's someone who wants to see you outside.' Now, this was just before warm-up, so I'm thinking, 'Who the hell wants to talk to me now?' So I go to the door and there's Brian Burke. He said, 'Watch out for Dave Brown! He's out to get you today! And he's a lefty.'

"Now, Dave Brown was *way* tougher than I was, and a big guy, and I didn't want anything to do with him. So now Brian Burke has me pissing my pants as we're going out for warm-ups! All I can think of is, 'Why me?' I've never even touched him or done anything to him. So the game starts and of course my head is on a swivel. The next thing I know, Brown is in a fight with Gord Kluzak. I think—good! That's good! At least he's not after me!

"I go back out and play a little more, and they get out of the penalty box, and Brown starts fighting Kluzak again! Okay! The game ends and I'm unscathed. Like, 35 years later Bobby Clarke comes to me and says, 'You know, I hated playing against you. I always wanted to get you. One day when we were playing at the Garden, I told Dave Brown to go after you, and he was supposed to take you out!'"

Now, as it turns out, Milbury's memory of that day against the Flyers coincided exactly with what Dave Brown told me about the game. The fact that Milbury was happy that Gord Kluzak had to fight Brown (twice!) and he didn't adds to his amusement. But it took him years to find out *why* Clarke wanted Brown to beat up Milbury. And Clarke admitted he tried to amp Brown up before the game.

"So I told Bobby Clarke, I heard about that. Brian Burke came and warned me before the game. So Clarke said, 'Well, Dave Brown was pissed at Gord Kluzak for something they had in juniors and he wanted to get even so he went after him instead of you!'

"When I played in the Canada Cup in 1976, which was prior to this incident, we were in an exhibition game with Team USA against Team Canada in Quebec City, and Bobby Clarke went to the front of the net to be the net-front presence—don't ask me why! Back then, as you know, you could use a hatchet on guys in front of the net, which I did! He turned around and dropped his gloves, and I split him open for a half dozen stitches, so I think he was still pissed about that."

Grudges die hard in the National Hockey League.

Milbury is from the Boston area and went on to play three years of varsity hockey at Colgate. In 76 college games for the Red Raiders, Mike had 61 points and 203 penalty minutes and, of course, led Colgate in penalty minutes in both his junior and senior seasons. But he was undrafted and had little hope for a hockey career after college. Fortunately, new Bruins coach Don Cherry had been told about Milbury and filed the information away.

"Grapes [Don Cherry] was in his first year as coach and they were going through the list at training camp, and he knew someone from Colgate who told him to keep an eye out for Milbury. So when the list was being put together, Grapes remembered that and I got a very late invitation to camp. But it was like, 'Who is this kid?' They didn't have a clue. Harry [Sinden] I'm sure never saw me play, Grapes had never seen me play at that point. I was just a walk-on, hope-and-a-prayer kind of tryout."

Milbury certainly did not come from a traditional collegiate hockey powerhouse, and in 1974 the deck was stacked against *any* player trying to make the jump from college to the NHL.

"I certainly did *not* arrive at training camp with any reputation," Milbury said. "I don't think there were many guys who knew who the f—k I was! I was undrafted. I had played a handful of games with the Boston Braves at the end of my senior year when they got so nicked up that had to call *me* up! I was one of four undrafted guys on the Bruins' 'negotiation list'—talk about indentured servitude, by the way! They put me on this list and suddenly they own my rights."

In 1974, Don Cherry was just starting the organizational culture that would produce the Big, Bad Bruins. He certainly had an idea of what kind of player he wanted and how that person should play the game—with snarl, attitude, and physicality. But, again, those are attributes not necessarily brought up when talking about college players.

"I would not say I came to the NHL as an 'American college tough guy,' although there were plenty of American college players who *were* tough," Milbury said. "And you had to be. My first training camp with the Bruins, I was in better shape than everybody. In those days, the veterans used training camp to get in shape, but I had stopped my job in August and was working out three or four times a day. When I got to camp, I was way ahead of everybody and there were actually guys telling me to slow down.

"I had a stick fight with Cashman in the first couple of days. To be honest, I was feeling a little isolated. There weren't many people who weren't Canadian in that lineup. There weren't many people from Europe and those that were, were abused. But I was big enough to handle myself and got through it."

The Don Cherry Bruins were following the mold originated by the Philadelphia Flyers. He wanted his team to be tough and together—if you fought one Bruin, you'd better be prepared to fight them all. But Milbury bristles at the notion that the only thing the Bruins could do back in those days was intimidate and fight.

"We certainly had one of the toughest teams ever, but I don't know if we could only have been successful if we played *that* way," Milbury said. "We certainly utilized that tactic, as was the style of the day, and it could be successful as it was for Philadelphia, and it certainly was for us but to a limited extent because we couldn't get past Montreal.

"If you look back at those Bruins teams, Wayne Cashman was a very productive player, Jean Ratelle was a Hall-of-Fame center ice man who could dish the puck, Nifty [Rick Middleton] probably should be in the Hall of Fame, Peter McNab was a 40-goal scorer, and Terry O'Reilly had 90 points one year. My point is, we were more talented than only being the Big, Bad Bruins. But we did embrace it."

But Milbury felt the Flyers did set the precedent for the time, and the Broad Street Bullies had success with that style of play, so it made sense to bring that same attitude to Boston. If ever a city was made to embrace that style of play, it was Boston.

"I think Bruins fans appreciate the try. I think they understand how much effort players put into it," Milbury said. "I'm not sure what the demographics are now, in terms of white collar and blue collar, but when I was playing there was a lot of blue-collar fans who could relate to the underdog status. They wanted to see players who achieved through visible signs of hard work, toughness, and hardscrabble. The lunch pail gang. Somebody gave us that moniker and it appealed not only to us but to everyone around New England that followed the Bruins."

Bruins fans loved that style and still do to this day. Tough guys are embraced by Bruins fans, perhaps beyond what their skills and talent level would justify. They are beloved when they play and long after their playing years. Terry O'Reilly has his No. 24 retired by the team. But for Milbury, it was probably a reaction to those two Flyers Stanley Cup championships.

"With the success of the Philadelphia Flyers, it meant we had to meet their level of ferocity in order to beat them," Milbury said. "The Flyers beat the Bruins a couple of times, including in a Stanley Cup Final before I was there, and in my first playoff season they beat us. They presented a very real physical challenge and an emotional challenge. We were generally tough enough and good enough to meet the Philadelphia challenge."

But if Milbury believes the Bruins were looking to emulate the style and success of the Flyers during that time period, he also acknowledges that it was the Montreal Canadiens who may have taught the Bruins the tougher lessons.

"We played them so often and lost to them so often, you had to take something from those defeats," Milbury said. "They were plenty tough, but they didn't have to resort to it as a tactic. They wanted to score goals and wins games, and if they were pinned in the corner they would fight back. But they didn't need that as part of their arsenal.

"We were very anxious to make sure that people didn't cross lines and if they did, we were going to fight them. But it doesn't always translate into a successful tactic. You find yourself in the box and if you make a mistake, you might even get beat up. But it doesn't translate into the ultimate, which is a win."

I mentioned to Milbury my observation about his teammate Terry O'Reilly—Terry, to this day, is one of the kindest, gentlest men I've ever met, but he had that ability to "flip the switch" when he was playing. Did Milbury feel he had a similar ability to "turn it on" when needed?

"I don't think I'm the kindest and gentlest human being, so we are very different people," Milbury said. "I like to think I know how to handle myself with some intelligence, but I can't say and Terry can't say that we didn't have our moments when our dark side revealed itself. That's true of both of us, I'm sure."

Mike started this discussion by talking about some of the people, even those in this book, he has fought. But there are others not named here who could be downright intimidating.

"Behn Wilson had these eyes that seemed to roll back in his head, where I actually think he lost control of himself, and that *anything* could happen," Milbury said. "There may have been tougher guys. Scott Stevens was another one who, when he was young, there was definitely a reason to be careful around him. There weren't as many restraints for those two guys as there seemed to be for the rest of us.

"John Wensink was in a fight in the American League, and he told me had his fingers behind a guy's eyeball and thought about whether he should pop out the eye or not. He decided against it. Heck, even John had restraints. Sort of."

Milbury was also an immediate eyewitness to another famous Big, Bad Bruins moment, when that same John Wensink challenged the entire Minnesota North Stars bench. They declined his invitation.

"I was 10 feet away to John's right. Don't ask me what I was doing there, but I was happy that they *didn't* all come out on the ice," Milbury said. "We would have been in trouble for a while until reinforcements came. The North Stars did take it to heart, and learn from it, and changed the physical makeup of their club going forward. But it's still a great moment, isn't it? The hands up, with the fingers gesturing, asking them to come off the bench, and then the disdainful wave at them when nobody comes! It *was* fun."

Mike's respect for O'Reilly is obvious. But he gets a little hesitant to anoint Terry (or any player) as the toughest to ever play.

"Taz was the most *determined* guy I ever played with, and he was the most righteous guy," Milbury said. "You couldn't cross the line against our team, not just against Terry, without him thinking he had to 'right the wrong.' But toughest? I don't know. I mean, Al Secord was one tough mother! Jay Miller was the same way. I don't really know to rank all these guys.

"Terry was a willing fighter, willing to take punches, willing to go the extra mile whenever he had to. But he didn't have great balance, for instance, and to be a great fighter you need to be able to get square. But he would go down swinging—literally! Don't get me wrong—he was a good fighter, a terrific fighter—but I would be hard-pressed to say he was the best fighter ever. But there was never any question about him answering the bell, no matter what condition he was in.' "

Mike and Terry were teammates, but they are also connected, perhaps forever, because of what took place on December 23, 1979, at Madison Square Garden. O'Reilly has his own recollection of the sequence of events that you can read elsewhere in this book. But for Milbury, it had always been a case of not even knowing exactly what happened or how he got involved.

"It was Madison Square Garden in the '70s and they were angry fans, nasty fans, and sometimes violent fans," Milbury said. "And they would always throw stuff—bottles, batteries, bolts, whatever! So Espo [Phil Esposito] had a breakaway with like 10 seconds left and Cheesie [Gerry Cheevers] stoned him, and some guy threw a tennis ball in front of Phil. We win, we have the group hug around the goaltender, and I go right out the Zamboni door at that end of the ice and head for the dressing room.

"This was two days before Christmas! The Budweiser was on ice, and everyone was ready to go home for a few days for the holidays. I was in a great mood; it was a terrific win against an archrival. Then nobody came into the dressing room. Finally, Cheesie came in and I think Nifty was with him, and I said, 'What's going on out there? Where is everybody?' And Cheesie told me there was some sort of beef out on the ice.

"I had already put down my stick and skates and was getting ready to get undressed, but I ran back out there. I looked up and my team was already in the stands! I had no idea why. And I had no reason to be angry, but I went from whistling a happy tune and going home for Christmas to my heart was racing a thousand miles an hour!"

What Milbury saw when he got out on the ice was a fracas involving his Bruins teammates in the stands at Madison Square Garden and at least one fan. Of all the players on that 1979 Bruins team, perhaps the one least likely to lead the charge was Peter McNab, but there he was.

"I could see Peter higher in the stands than everyone else, and we sat beside each other in the locker room, so I figured I had to go give him a hand," Milbury said. "Peter already had the guy reversed over the seats and his feet were over the back of a chair sticking up in the air. At the time I remembered it differently than when I saw it on tape. I thought the guy was flailing wildly, but he actually just flicked his leg out, and I grabbed his leg and grabbed his shoe and hit him over the thigh.

"It certainly wasn't pre-planned, and I didn't even know what this guy had done or why Peter was wrestling with him. Hell, I didn't know what I was doing there! But it quickly became A Thing! For the next three days it was plastered all over the news, when there were only three stations, and it was everywhere! I remember doing interview after interview in that time frame."

The NHL and commissioner John Ziegler came down hard on the Bruins. Three players, including Mike, were suspended, and that decision was upheld even after the team appealed the punishments and was granted a hearing.

"I think Ziegler described my actions as 'despicable,'" Milbury said. "There was a hearing and there was a split vote whether to uphold Ziegler's suspension ruling or not. But in the end, there were enough people who thought that if they overruled Ziegler it would have been the end of them, and they didn't want to go that far.

"Taz got eight games and Peter and I were suspended for six games. At the time, I certainly didn't think I deserved to be suspended for that long. There were guys lower in the stands than me who were throwing some serious haymakers at the fans. A lot of guys down below told me they were doing a number on people.

"I will tell you that going up in the stands was kind of a macho feeling for me, because everyone just sort of got out of the way! I was 6'2", and 6'5" on skates, so they weren't as brave when we were going into the stands as they were when we were on the ice.

"I didn't think I deserved what I got, but I had to see the tape to even know what brought this whole thing on. I clearly was not part of the beginning of the thing, and I don't know what I was thinking. I just had to go help teammates who were in the middle of 15,000 Rangers fans and under some threat, so that's what I did."

When I worked in the American Hockey League in the early '80s, bench-clearing brawls were the norm. I don't want to make it sound like it happened every game, but it was not unusual to see two or even three brawls in a week. As much as I enjoyed calling hockey fights, I never liked seeing bench-clearing brawls. While I thought it was unlikely that a player would be severely injured in a fight (and I'm not sure how correct that feeling was), I felt like players could easily get injured in a bench-clearing brawl. It was just too hard to properly defend yourself.

It wasn't until 1987 and the famous Montreal Canadiens–Philadelphia Flyers playoff pregame debacle that the NHL finally made moves to rid the game of bench-clearing brawls. They certainly didn't happen every game, but they were a fairly regular occurrence, and Milbury admits that being in one is something that is hard to forget.

"Being in a bench-clearing brawl was an amazing thing. It was like being in an actual street fight," Milbury said. "You don't know where people are coming from, you don't know who's gonna hit you, you don't know whether to duck and cover or just keep flailing away. It was a crazy thing to be in those brawls.

"I know, as a participant, I'll never forget them. I wasn't in very many of them, but they were just wild events that sear your memory. And I'm sure it did for fans. I can remember throwing haymakers at unsuspecting players. I can remember getting thrown at. Was I scared? Sure, I was. But over steak and brew later, it also made for a bonding moment for a team."

But as the years went on, and Mike moved from playing to coaching to managing, he began to view fighting differently. Like many others in and around the sport, he began to wonder whether it was smart to allow it and what the long-term consequences might be.

"My 'come to Jesus' moment was when we started to hear about the long-term impact of concussions," Milbury said. "Whether I liked it or not, it seemed to me prudent to take a different approach. First of all, with helmets and visors, it's becoming less and less dangerous in the normal way to fight. But you could still smack a guy and a concussion is caused by the torque of snapping a guy's neck and head. It became common sense to me that it was time to let it go. I felt it was an ineffective part of the game."

This caused some internal conflict for Milbury, who had been a part of one of the toughest teams of all time but was beginning to wonder if fighting should still be allowed. His ambivalence dated back to his early experiences.

"Now, don't get me wrong—I love the vigilantism, I love when someone does something wrong and you can be the judge and the jury, and you could take matters into your own fists, and try to right the wrong," Milbury said. "It was fun to see that happen, but it got to the point where everybody was doing it just to try and scare people and get them away from playing hockey. It was at that point it became a little silly. That's the stuff we had to get away from.

"I understood the genesis of the Flyers. They got beat up by St. Louis and Ed Snider said it was never gonna happen to his team again, and it didn't. But it became kind of *Slap Shot*-ish. But not so *Slap Shot*-ish that they didn't win two Stanley Cups doing it."

This was a discussion I had also had on many occasions with Bruins general manager Harry Sinden. Sinden felt the sport had to evolve past fighting if it entertained any hope of growing the fan base beyond just hard-core hockey fans. It's not a fear Milbury shares.

"Our sport is so expensive to play, it's so hard to get ice time, and so I don't know that we're ever gonna be anything more than a niche sport," Milbury said. "But we've got a wide enough niche to be successful. Someone told me the other day you can be on the Toronto Maple Leafs season ticket waiting list for 30 years! They have a 99.5 percent season ticket return rate, which is remarkable. It says something about the depth of passion of fans, especially in Toronto. I never thought that eliminating fighting was ever going to exponentially grow the sport; in fact, we might lose people who enjoy fighting."

The other argument about allowing fighting in hockey—and one I've made many times myself—is that it allows self-policing and prevents worse actions. If you don't fear having to answer for your stick work, for instance, will it ultimately make the sport even *more* dangerous?

Again, Milbury isn't so sure.

"It's a good question. There are those who espouse that the reduction in fighting emboldens players to do different things than they might if they had to answer for their actions. I don't think it's made that much of a difference. I still think there's a way to even the score in hockey without a fight. You can look for a hit, you can look to intimidate by making sure the other guy *knows* you're going to hit him. I don't believe a player thinks, 'I'll high-stick this guy because there's no more fighting.' I don't think there's a conscious cause and effect there. But I will say there's some limitations on people's behavior with fighting than without."

The bottom line for Milbury—and it's always about the bottom line for Milbury—is that fighting in the sport not only isn't necessary anymore but is actually "ludicrous" to continue to allow.

"It's Neanderthal to allow it, when we know that there have been guys—Bob Probert comes to mind, and I know he had other issues—who have had their brains rattled around in their skulls repeatedly, and that can lead to serious problems," Milbury said. "And generally speaking, the fights aren't any good anymore anyways. They really don't serve a lot of purpose, and there's no intimidation in the game because of fighting.

"It's silly, and I don't see why Gary Bettman and others can't see their way clear to eliminate fighting from the game. Are they worried people might not buy as many tickets? There is the odd good fight, but it really sticks out now. But what does fighting do to a guy, long term? We don't really know, but I don't think that it's worth it. It's time—it's just time to get rid of it. It's time to mature and time to grow up."

Milbury goes even further—if he were suddenly made NHL commissioner for a day, fighting would be eliminated immediately.

"I definitely would. What other sport even allows it?" Milbury said. "There's an occasional bench-clearing pushing match in baseball, but no real fighting. Football doesn't allow fighting, and you almost never see it in that sport. Basketball just isn't interested in it. It doesn't exist anywhere else.

"It's been part of the game, and I've loved the immediacy of meting out justice when it needed to be meted out. I've loved the fact that you could do it yourself, and you didn't have to wait for someone else to do it. I've loved the fact that it charges people up. I get all of that, I got all of that and I lived all of that, but now I believe it's just a matter of making sure people not only can play hockey for a living but can leave the game without having to pay even more of a price than they already do. They should be able to go golfing or play with their grandchildren if they want to.

"I don't believe there would be an effect on the fan base of the sport. Oh, there would be some people growling about it, but it's already been so reduced. If you think about what we were doing in the '70s, there's none of that in today's game anymore. Now, you can intimidate with your speed and with your body contact, and you don't need fighting anymore. And in the end, in the Stanley Cup Final, there's no room for it at all. You can't afford to take a penalty; you can't afford to be the guy that puts his team shorthanded and winds up with a power-play goal against that might decide things. As the games increase in importance, fighting is reduced in significance."

I remember vividly an argument I had with Milbury when he was coaching the Bruins. Milbury said he wanted Hall of Fame power forward Cam Neely to fight less. My assertion was it was Neely's fighting ability that helped give him the extra room to be a prolific 50-goal scorer in the NHL. Milbury was having none of that either.

"Cam Neely got the room he did because he was that big and that strong and could skate that well," Milbury said. "Did he get a little extra room from some guys because he might start pumping those left hands at them? Sure. But I didn't think he needed it to be as successful as he was."

Milbury is sometimes a lightning rod in the sport. He says what he thinks and means what he says. There have been times when his willingness to shoot from the hip has gotten him in trouble.

On March 30, 1994, Boston College announced that Milbury would replace Steve Cedorchuk as head coach for the legendary Eagles hockey program. Less than three months later, the college announced that Mike was leaving the program, citing "philosophical differences." He never coached a game at the Heights. (By the way, Boston College hired Jerry York to replace Milbury as head coach, and I guess his 656 career wins for the Eagles and four national championships means they made the right choice.)

Milbury has been criticized on several occasions for comments he made while serving as a commentator. He ran into difficulties with fans in Nashville for ranting about P. K. Subban. He said he believed Toronto Maple Leafs defenseman Jake Muzzin was faking an injury prior to Muzzin being carted off the ice on a stretcher. He criticized Tuukka Rask for leaving the Covid bubble for the Stanley Cup playoffs due to a medical situation involving Rask's daughter. Milbury ultimately stepped away from his job with NBC Sports during the playoffs in August 2020 so he would not be a distraction. The following January, NBC elected to not bring him back for its final season of telecasting NHL hockey.

Milbury is back in the Boston area and working for several different media outlets. As always, he is never afraid to have an opinion.

It's always thought-provoking to have a hockey discussion with Mike Milbury. He challenges you to make your argument, be able to back up your opinion, and be willing to spar. This book has largely focused on not only the tough guys who have made our sport so great, but on the possible toll it takes on the men who play that way. I'm not saying that any opinion is more valid than any other, but I've at least tried to open my mind to other possibilities.

Just don't ask Mike Milbury a question if you don't want to hear the answer.

CHAPTER 10

BRIAN BURKE

B RIAN BURKE DOESN'T court conflict—though he may have taken it on a date or two. He also never runs from it, choosing to handle it like he's handled his entire life—head-on and no quarter taken. Conflict seems to follow Burke around from time to time, and he is unapologetic for his feelings and beliefs. For instance, he thinks there should be *more* fighting in hockey, not less. And he has no problem backing up those beliefs. He's the man who introduced the word *truculence* to describe his preferred brand of hockey. That made him perfect to interview for this project.

Burke might also have one of the most eclectic résumés in hockey. He played collegiate hockey at Providence College for Lou Lamoriello and was captain of the team his senior year. One of his teammates and lifelong friends was Ron Wilson. He and Wilson were born a month apart and Burke, as loyal a person as I've ever met, hired Wilson as his coach with the Toronto Maple Leafs—and gave him a controversial midseason contract extension despite three consecutive losing seasons. Burke played just a year of professional hockey at the minor league level in the Philadelphia Flyers organization, then decided he needed to choose a different career path.

The training ground at Providence was perfect for Burke. Lamoriello has forged a spectacular career. His New Jersey Devils won three Stanley Cup championships, and Lamoriello has been inducted into the United States Hockey Hall of Fame and the Hockey Hall of Fame in the builders category. The four years that Burke spent playing for Lamoriello had to have been priceless to prepare Burke for his own hockey management career. And Lamoriello was always known for favoring physical, intimidating teams.

Burke went on to Harvard Law School, earning his JD in 1981 and becoming a player agent. Burke got to know Pat Quinn when Quinn was coaching in the Flyers organization, and Quinn hired Burke to serve as director of hockey operations for the Vancouver Canucks. He spent a season as general manager for the Hartford Whalers before leaving to work for the NHL as executive vice president and director of hockey operations. Part of his duties involved serving as the chief disciplinary officer.

Burke went on to serve as general manager of the Vancouver Canucks, Anaheim Ducks, and Toronto Maple Leafs. He also served in upper management for the Calgary Flames and most recently served as president of hockey operations for the Pittsburgh Penguins. He was also the general manager for the U.S. Olympic hockey team at the 2010 Winter Games in Vancouver. In other words, Burke has done it all. Even if he did get a very late start in the game.

"I started hockey so late—I didn't start playing until I was 13 years old—and I set my four rules, which I also wrote in my book [*Burke's Law*]," Burke said. "Rule No. 1 was I would always be the hardest worker. No. 2, I would be a coach's dream. No. 3 was I would be an ideal teammate. And No. 4 was I would always play tough. So physical hockey was always a priority for me even before I got to Providence College. Hell, that was how I made the team, because I banged as much as I could."

Like others I've spoken to for this book who played collegiately before turning pro, Burke was forced to play a game that automatically ejected a player for fighting. But the lack of fighting did *not* mean you could not play a very physical style of play.

"We didn't have that rule that prohibited body contact that might also involve the head," Burke said. "If you really dumped a guy, but maybe made contact with his head, officials could decide if it contributed at all to the penalty. As long as you kept your shoulder down and finished the guy, it was legal. If you make a full-length body check and hit a guy who is cutting through the middle, you're going to make some contact with his head, even if it's secondary or tertiary. That's something that has been eliminated that I think we should allow."

After completing his collegiate career, Burke played seven games for the Springfield Indians of the American Hockey League. It was, as Burke would admit, less than ideal.

"Springfield was a weird situation because we split the franchise with the Washington Capitals. The Washington guys just had a different mindset than the Flyers guys. The next year, the Flyers put their own franchise in Portland, Maine, and I thought it was very important that we had all Flyers players together.

The Flyers' mindset was very much alive. We were built in the image of the Broad Street Bullies, and I'm pretty sure we led the American Hockey League in fighting majors that year. That style of play became part of our trademark."

The entire Flyers ethos dated back to the 1967–68 and 1968–69 seasons when the Flyers not only lost to the St. Louis Blues but were emasculated by them. The story has always been that team owner Ed Snider vowed it would never happen to his team again.

"That is absolutely, one hundred percent true," Burke said. "It's the only story I've ever heard. Pat Quinn told me about that way back in the day. It wasn't just Mr. Snider, but the general manager, Keith Allen, had the exact same mindset. We were never going to get pushed around again—*ever!* Certainly not in Philly."

The Philadelphia Flyers transformed into the Broad Street Bullies, and the first and only professional season that Burke played was in that organization. He played for the Maine Mariners, who went on to capture the AHL Calder Cup championship in their first year of existence. The Mariners were, to put it mildly, a *very* physical hockey team. They had five players top 100 minutes in penalties and, as Burke remembers, they led the AHL in fighting majors that season. Burke has always believed in playing physical hockey, but the Mariners reinforced that idea for him.

Burke learned quickly that he was not going to make a living as a player in the NHL and became a player agent. In the Mike Milbury chapter, you might recall Burke meeting with Milbury at the Bruins' dressing room door to warn him that Dave Brown was out to get him in the game that night. How did Burke know this?

"I knew because Dave Brown was a client of mine," Burke said. "I would *never* disclose secrets of any of my guys. Like, if

Brownie had a bad right hand, I would never pass that along, but after David told me he was going to get Milbury, I thought I better let him know. To me that wasn't tipping him off to anything. I liked Mike."

You'll recall that Brown ended up fighting Gord Kluzak twice that game and never fought Milbury, despite Bobby Clarke's urging. But that very idea of carrying a grudge, and settling a score, is something Burke appreciates.

"I love that about our game," Burke said. "Trevor Linden's first year in the NHL, he speared a guy. And I said to him afterward, 'Trev, we don't play that way here.' He said, 'That guy ran me my first day of training camp when I was a rookie [three years earlier], and I've just been waiting to get him!'

"I remember fighting Dave Lumley. When I was a junior in college and Dave was a senior, he speared me. Two years later in the American Hockey League, we played against him and I fought him as soon as I got on the ice with him. That's an endearing thing to me. Guys do settle scores and they do keep track."

It was interesting that NHL commissioner Gary Bettman hired Burke to serve as league disciplinarian in 1993. A guy who not only liked fighting but staunchly advocated in favor of it was now going to decide who did or didn't cross the line. But Burke was also adamant that his feelings about how the game *should* be played would not be a factor in getting the job with the league.

"When I interviewed for the job with Gary Bettman, I told him that if there wasn't a clear vision for our sport that included physicality, then I wasn't interested," Burke said. "Gary assured me that we wanted physicality. I hope we never lose that, and I think we never will. I think there's a big difference between crossing the line and being physical. We want hitting, we prize hitting, we celebrate body contact. We just want to make sure that when players cross the line, we act appropriately. I was the guy that decided what was safe for hockey players and what wasn't."

It is also interesting that other particularly physical players have served in similar roles for the NHL. Brendan Shanahan accumulated nearly 2,500 penalty minutes over his career and triple-digit penalties 17 times in his 21 NHL seasons. He was the director of player safety for the league and began the system of making public videos that completely broke down the disciplinary action he took on behalf of the league for every player suspended.

George Parros, like Burke, also played four years of college hockey. He was also captain of his Princeton University team in his senior year. Parros majored in economics at Princeton and wrote about the West Coast longshoremen's dispute for his senior thesis. Like Burke, Parros believed strongly in the advantages of physical hockey. He had 247 penalty minutes for the Manchester Monarchs of the American Hockey League in 2004–05, triple-digit penalties in six NHL seasons, and 1,092 penalty minutes in 474 career games. Now he is head of the Department of Player Safety.

It should come as no surprise Burke liked and appreciated players like George Parros. In fact, when Burke was general manager of the Anaheim Ducks, he built a team after his own image. And the result was a Stanley Cup championship.

"Our Cup team with the Ducks had top defensemen, highly skilled players in the top six forwards, great goaltending, but a lot of physical play," Burke said. "Shawn Thornton, Brad May, George Parros, Sean O'Donnell, and Francois Beauchemin made us a very tough team. No one's won the Cup with a tougher team since we won it."

In fact, Brian says one of his biggest regrets came the summer after that Stanley Cup title, when he failed to keep a big part of the team's physical core.

"One of the biggest mistakes I made as a general manager was not re-signing Shawn Thornton when I was with Anaheim," Burke said. "He got a three-year deal from Boston, and I wouldn't go past two years, and it was a horrible loss for us."

It is also a particular point of pride for Burke that he built a big, physical team and proved you could win a Stanley Cup that way. In fact, Brian thinks he may have shown the rest of the NHL the blueprint to winning—get big and get physical.

"I thought that St. Louis Blues team that beat the Bruins in the Stanley Cup Final was the closest team to our Ducks championship team," Burke said. "That Blues team was a big, mean team and I thought they played the right way. I think it's a critical part. The two Penguins Cups were probably the last teams to win small, but every championship team since then has been big."

Legendary Bowdoin College hockey coach Sid Watson once told me that NCAA was making a huge mistake when it made the full cage mandatory in the game. He feared the cage would make players fearless and create little tanks who did not think they could hurt others or be hurt.

The question for me was: Did the instigator penalty do the same thing? Did it make players braver than they might normally be, knowing opponents would be hesitant to be tagged with the extra instigator penalty?

"There is no question that putting the cage on college hockey made players more fearless. I agree completely with Sid on that," Burke said. "But when it comes to the instigator penalty, I have to say this about the officials. They've become very judicious about how they assess that penalty. It's only assessed about 20 percent of the time, but you could argue there could be an instigator penalty 60 to 80 percent of the time. I think the officials have done a good job in enforcing that cautiously. For that reason, I don't think the instigator penalty is causing other problems.

"We want players to go after other guys in certain instances. When a goalie gets run over and someone goes after the guilty party? We want that! That's how we police the game. I didn't like the instigator penalty. It was put in as a compromise, to try and get rid of fighting. I didn't like it, and I still don't like it."

That compromise was put in place, in part, to counter those in NHL management positions who felt that fighting should be eliminated completely from the game. Bruins general manager Harry Sinden, for instance, felt the game would never gain complete acceptance until fighting was banned, as it is in other sports. To put it simply, Burke disagrees with Sinden and those who share his view.

"Harry and I have had that discussion going back to when I worked for the National Hockey League," Burke said. "We had a general managers meeting and I got stuck at a table with Mike Smith, Serge Savard, and Harry Sinden. They were all 'Greenpeace Guys' and saying we had to get rid of fighting. I told them they had all lost their f—ing minds! So I've had the discussion with Harry. I don't agree and I never will agree. I'm not one of those guys who got religion late. A lot of guys, later in life, turn on fighting. They say we've got to get rid of fighting. I'm not like that."

Don't misunderstand Burke here—after the 1987 Stanley Cup pregame brawl between the Flyers and the Canadiens, the NHL put rules in place that effectively ended the bench-clearing brawl. And that was fine with Brian.

"I had no problems getting rid of bench-clearing brawls. I don't think three-hour games were good for our sport," Burke said. "I don't think bench-clearing brawls and seven or eight fights in a game was a good thing. I'm talking about having a fight, maybe two, in a rough game and maybe three in a *really* rough game. I'm not talking about going back to what it was like when I turned pro with the Maine Mariners. I'm not a dinosaur. I don't yearn for the old days when we had a fight every five minutes. I don't mind that we eliminated bench-clearing brawls."

But as medical science has greatly expanded our knowledge about head injuries, head trauma, and CTE, many *have* been rethinking the idea of fighting in hockey. But for Burke, that knowledge has perhaps helped keep players safer now than they were in years past.

"The issue with head injuries is we didn't know what they were and how to deal with them. Now we do," Burke said. "We certainly have to be careful and utilize the best medical science available. We are talking about contact sports. Did the NFL do away with kickoffs? They didn't change the rules to eliminate hitting in football; they just got rid of the egregious head shots. UFC is the fastest-growing sport in the last 20 years, and guess what? They hit! I don't want to change the game. The women's game in hockey is a fantastic game, really great, and they don't allow hitting. But I don't want to see that in our game."

The college game and international play are a big part of Burke's résumé, and fighting is not allowed as a part of the game in either venue. But don't think for a minute that Burke finds his admiration for both those versions of hockey and the NHL hypocritical.

"There *is* fighting in Olympic hockey, but you get ejected," Burke said. "There's no fighting in college hockey. I have no problem with the game under those conditions. But that doesn't mean we need that same set of rules to apply in the NHL. There's a lot of things about the Olympics that are ridiculous! We don't have to parrot or exactly copy everything about Olympic hockey. We shouldn't emulate the Olympics. If they don't want to allow fighting, that's fine."

The United States' overtime loss in the gold medal game in Vancouver is considered by many as one of the great deciding games in Olympic history. The winning Canadian team was a veritable who's who of hockey talent. The American silver medalists were considered a vastly inferior team but ended up losing the gold medal on a Sidney Crosby overtime goal.

"Keep in mind we were picked to finish sixth in those games, and we ended losing in overtime in the gold medal game," Burke said. "International hockey has been a wonderful part of my life, and the Vancouver games were the highlight and the lowlight. I've never felt lower than I did after we lost that gold medal game. I love the Olympics and I love international hockey, and neither allows fighting. What does one thing have to with the other? And keep this in mind about the Olympics. The only real way to crown a champion is a best-of-three or best-of-seven series, not a one-and-done."

Burke has always admired players like the ones featured in this book, and he always will. He knows better than most how difficult the job is and also understands how important those players are to the sport. He also knows how much tough guys are admired by their teammates.

"If you think about the guys you're writing about in this book, they're all good guys," Burke said. "They're all popular team-mates, they're all active in the community, and they're all really well liked. But you're also dealing with a spectrum of players too. Terry O'Reilly was a great hockey player who just happened to be really tough. Some of the other guys you might remember more because they were just tough. O'Reilly was a hell of a player; Jay Miller was a guy who could play forward or defense, although maybe a bit of a wing nut. Perhaps the characters in the game were a bit more interesting back then. But everyone gravitates toward these guys. First, it's the toughest job to do, so teammates like and respect those guys.

"My theory was always that the charisma and character of tough guys allows them to not be a villain. They're trying so hard to be popular, so people don't think they're bad guys. The other part is that it's their release. If they're going to play that hard and do that job—which is so frigging tough!—it's a release for them to be charming and to be mostly graceful. There is not one tough guy I've ever met who was not a nice person."

But a common trait among those "nice" people is the ability to be not so nice in a heartbeat. Dave Brown, Archie Henderson, Terry O'Reilly, and others may well be among the easiest people to deal with off the ice, but on the ice they also had the ability to become something completely different.

"Players like that do have an ability to flip a switch when they need to," Burke said. "Guys like Dave Brown, who did that job for a living, held down the hardest job in pro sports. It takes a toll on guys. But that's also why those guys are such popular teammates. You've got to be able to turn it on and off. When I first turned pro, I was talking to my dad and I said, 'I've got to learn to get mad fast!' I've got a horrible temper, but I've got a long fuse. And part of the formula for successful fighters is getting mad fast."

Chris Nilan talked about warning his Canadiens teammates that he was going to start something out on the ice. He wanted to be ready to respond when it happened and to lift their emotional level when called upon. Burke thinks Chris is on to something.

"Physical play and intimidation is contagious," Burke said. "But fear and toughness can both be contagious. You can see fear infiltrate a team and a dressing room if you don't have a proper response. You can see it happen. But the same thing goes for toughness. Toughness and fear are both transferable skills."

Matt Cooke delivered an egregious hit on Bruins star forward Marc Savard. The two teams didn't know it at the time, but the hit effectively ended Savard's career. When the two teams got together in their next meeting, Shawn Thornton told Pittsburgh's Bill Guerin before the game that Matt Cooke *had* to fight Thornton in response to his hit on Savard.

Thornton said if Cooke stepped up, on his very first shift, the situation would be handled, and the game's great players could play the way they should. If the altercation did not take place,

Patrice Bergeron and Sidney Crosby would have to spend the entire game with their heads on a swivel, awaiting a physical response that would be certain with highlights that would be splashed all over *SportsCenter* that night for all the wrong reasons. Thornton said the game would be a bloodbath.

To his credit, Cooke responded. He and Thornton fought, the situation was taken care of, and the game went on as it should. The players had policed the game themselves and handled things the proper way. Thornton and his teammates could not undo the damage done to Savard, but they did the best they could under the circumstances.

"I think to be a great player you have to have a level of fear-lessness," Burke said. "All great players find a way to excel despite the physical risks inherent in our sport, whether they're on a tough team or not. [The Pittsburgh Penguins] don't fight a lot, and that doesn't affect the way Sid plays at all. But we expect our teammates to back Sid up too when he needs it."

I had a friend who once said he would like to have the physical abilities of the *worst* player in Major League Baseball history because that player was better than him or anyone he had ever played with. Fans who don't think *every* player in the game has to have a certain level of physical toughness and courage have never played the game. Burke knows that they do.

I have admitted to having changing thoughts about fighting in the National Hockey League. I have seen the physical toll it's taken on certain players, and I still have my doubts about our depth of knowledge concerning trauma and CTE. But talking with Brian Burke also provides an alternate view of that aspect of the game. He makes the case that the game is better with fighting than without and that fans want that physical aspect of the sport to remain.

"I used to say to myself before going on the ice every time—practice or games—'Make it good because this could be it,'" Burke said. "You could lose an eye or blow out a knee at any time. That was my credo that I said before going on the ice every single time. You're playing a contact sport, so you're taking risks. You've got to be willing to run those risks."

For Brian Burke, life is very simple—say what you mean and mean what you say. Treat people like you would want to be treated. Don't be afraid to hold unpopular positions and always be willing to back them up. And spend your life doing what you love.

"My advice to anyone who gets involved in sports is to have a creed, have a code, that you live by and don't ever change," Burke said. "You have to adapt, but that's not the same thing as changing. The game of hockey has adapted. Fighting and its role has decreased substantially over the years, and maybe that's a good thing. But I do think we've gone too far. I would like to see some more fighting in the game. You can adapt over time, like with analytics. You adapt or you die. But I also think you should have a basic code on how you treat people, how you act, what is right and wrong. That should never change; it will certainly never change for me."

CHAPTER 11

MATTHEW BARNABY

———

IN THE INTEREST OF FULL DISCLOSURE, I know virtually every person I spoke to for this project. I have been friends for nearly 40 years with some of them and have had professional relationships with almost everyone else.

So, I felt like I needed to step outside my comfort zone. I needed to talk with someone I didn't know—and more importantly, I needed to talk with someone I didn't like. My publisher helped make a connection for me, and I went into my initial conversation with this player with a predetermined idea of what he was like. I didn't appreciate him at all.

I had certainly seen him play, had called some of his fights, and felt like he was a jerk on and off the ice. I had read about some of his issues away from the game (but outside the scope of this book) and felt no sympathy for him whatsoever. In fact, to the contrary, what I had read about him simply reinforced my impressions of him as a player and a person.

Then something strange happened. I talked with Matthew Barnaby—and I liked him.

Our first conversations started on a rocky note. I live in Maine and Matthew lives in upstate New York, and I don't know if you've heard, but the weather is not always perfect in those two areas. We arranged for a phone interview and happened to hit a day when it was storming both in Maine and New York. As a result, our internet connection was spotty at best, and we kept getting disconnected until it became clear it just wasn't going to happen.

I texted Matthew and apologized for the connection issues (as if I had any control over the weather), fully expecting this might put an end to this chapter of the book. What I got in return was a simple text: "Hey, no problem! Let's connect early next week." We did, and I was happy we did.

Matthew Barnaby was born in Ottawa, Ontario, and was the product of a single-parent household. He was raised by his mom and appreciated at an early age the sacrifices she made to allow him to pursue his athletic dreams.

"My mom always made it possible for me to play whatever sport I wanted," Barnaby said. "And hockey is expensive, so it was difficult for her to find the resources we needed. But she always did. She worked full time and always found the money for equipment or tournament fees. I played whatever sport was in season, and she made it all possible."

Matthew was hoping he would get drafted into the Quebec Major Junior Hockey League, but it was certainly not a given. In fact, he left the draft after the 15th round, disappointed and disillusioned because he'd felt he would have an opportunity before then. He wasn't even there to hear his name called by the Beaufort Harfangs.

"Beaufort drafted me in the last and 20th round," Barnaby said. "I guess I was Mr. Irrelevant, and it certainly gave me the impression they had no real hopes for me as a player. My brother told me I had to do something to get noticed, and that's what I decided to do. I was 17 years old and weighed less than 150 pounds, but I thought the way I could get noticed was to fight. I had something like 13 fights in the first three days of training camp. The coach decided he was going to keep me around, and I had my chance."

Matthew played 52 games that first season for Beaufort and had nine goals, 14 points, and 262 penalty minutes. He had found a way to get noticed, but he also realized he had to get bigger and stronger if he was going to continue to play that way.

He worked hard in the offseason and was able to put some weight and muscle definition on his young frame. The results spoke for themselves. In his second season he played in 63 games with 29 goals, 37 assists, 66 points, and a whopping 476 penalty minutes.

"I wasn't really thinking that it was my NHL draft year; I was playing day-to-day and game-to-game, doing anything I could do to help my team and keep my spot on the ice," Barnaby said. "I fought a lot that year, but I honestly think I only won a fight or two out of the 50 or so I had. Remember, I had been a real player going into the Quebec League. I had scored 43 goals in 50 games playing for Hull the season before my junior draft year. But I had to do what I had to do to stick and that meant being a pest and sticking up for my teammates."

If you spend any time talking with Matthew, the word *team-mate* comes up a lot. And the word "good" is almost always in front of it. If you ask him what it means to him to be a good teammate, he doesn't even hesitate.

"Being a good teammate, honestly, just meant bringing 110 percent every night, and standing up for my teammates," Barnaby said. "I think that was paramount in my role. Every night I had to bring everything I had, even if it was on a back-to-back or you were tired or playing through injury. In that era, I had to stand up for teammates who might have been taken advantage of."

As a result of getting noticed that season in Beaufort, Matthew was drafted by the Buffalo Sabres in the fourth round, 83rd overall in 1992. He had the chance to continue to chase his dream and play at the next level.

He spent one last season playing in the Quebec League, splitting the year between Beaufort, Verdun, and Victoriaville. But if you add his numbers from those three stops, he played in 65 games, with 44 goals, 67 assists, 111 points, and a whopping 448 penalty minutes. That meant in two full seasons in the QMJHL, he had amassed 924 penalty minutes in just 128 games.

"I don't care what level you're playing at; that's a lot of penalty minutes!" Barnaby said. "But to me, it just meant I was there for my teammates when they needed me."

Matthew carried that same style of play into the pros. He had 259 penalty minutes his first season and 390 in his second, splitting both years between the Rochester Americans of the American Hockey League and the Buffalo Sabres. In 1995 he made the jump to the NHL for good and never looked back.

It was that 1995–96 Sabres team that had to give opposing teams nightmares. They weren't very good, going 33–42–7–0 under head coach Ted Nolan. They certainly had some high-end talent, with Pat LaFontaine scoring 40 goals, but that Sabres team was more known for team toughness from front to back.

Matthew led the team with 335 penalty minutes, and teammates Brad May and Rob Ray added 295 and 287, respectively. Playing against that Sabres team that season could be a war, and while Barnaby led the way, those guys were willing co-stars.

"We had a pretty tough team," Barnaby said. "We also had guys like Brent Hughes and Bob Boughner on that team too. We had a *lot* of guys who were willing every single night. We weren't very good, and I've had guys tell me over the years, 'You know, we probably could have blown you out a little more, but we were afraid of what you knuckleheads were going to do!' It was a fun team to play on, and I think it set the tone for what our team was going to be known as. We wanted to be known as the hardest-working team in hockey. It started with team toughness, then we added some skill along the way. But playing with those guys made my job a hell of a lot easier, that's for sure!"

You've probably seen photos of fighters in that era of the NHL's history. When Dave Brown fought Chris Nilan in that pregame playoff brawl in 1987, he came out of the dressing room with nothing on up top. He put on his elbow pads as he came to the ice, in case he fell on the ice, but entered the arena with no shoulder pads and no jersey on. There are many photos of Matthew after a fight down to nothing but a T-shirt.

"Rob Ray was the master of it," Barnaby said. "He attached his jersey to his shoulder pads so any tug, and he could slide right out. Trust me—fighting a guy with nothing to hold on to is very dangerous. There is nothing to grab onto and to gain some leverage against. Rob was the best, but when the rule changes took that away, we started to do things like cut lines down our jerseys and put velcro in, so when someone tugged the jersey it just pulled right away. Then we started wearing goalie-cut jerseys so guys couldn't grab hold of your arms, they only got the jersey. No matter what the NHL came up with, the criminals were always going to find a way to gain an advantage. The game is certainly different today, but back then was like the Wild, Wild West!"

That Sabres team was truly "all for one and one for all." It was the style of play that best suited Matthew, and how he felt team-mates should be. And for tough guys, that meant never taking a night off and never being allowed to have a bad game. Some tough guys have talked about the fear of letting teammates down, but Barnaby had different concerns.

"I never feared it from the perspective of letting my team-mates down," Barnaby said. "I approached every game like it was my last, and I never *wanted* to let my teammates down. But I didn't fear that I was was *going* to let them down. I just knew that I was going to do everything I possibly could for that team and those players, and those fans I was playing in front of in my city.

"But I *did* want the guys in that room to know I would do anything—I would take punches in the face for them, I was going to take slashes. Because of the way I played, I was going to draw penalties, and everything that I did was calculated to give my team an edge, in either getting a power play or getting opponents off their game. I just wanted them to know I was always willing to take those bumps and bruises for the betterment of the team."

If you watch a fight between legitimate NHL tough guys, usually the first thing that jumps out at you is the violence. Fighters seem to go from zero to 60 in seconds, and it always appears there is real animosity between the combatants. Did that mean Barnaby had to "fight mad"—that he had to be seriously upset at the person he was going to punch in the face? Believe it or not, his answer is no.

"No, I did not have to fight mad," Barnaby said. "When I went into a fight, I was smaller than most of the guys I was fighting against, and I had to go in with a strategic plan. When I went into a fight, I didn't have to be mad, I just had to be ready. I had to know who I was fighting and how I needed to fight that person, like was he a lefty or a righty. I couldn't let my emotions get the best of me and leave a spot open, because guys were too big and hit too hard. If I was angry and exposed my chin, that could end a career pretty quickly."

Most (but not all) NHL tough guys do play by a certain set of rules—even if it doesn't look like it. Shawn Thornton and others have called it The Code, and the specifics may be different from player to player. There is nothing written out and nothing set in stone, but most guys try to abide by their own rules.

"Everyone asks me about a code, and I don't know if I had an actual code or just an appreciation for how hard it is to do what we were doing," Barnaby said. "The only 'code' I ever had, and I think most guys had it too, was what to do when a guy went down. When I watched hockey in the '70s, if a guy went down, opponents would just jump on them and keep punching them in the face. The code I lived by was if I had a guy down, I stopped. I always knew I might be in that similar place someday, and I would hope I would be given the same consideration. You can be down and unable to defend yourself, and that's when you can get seriously hurt. Everyone had certain rules that they lived by, but that was the one big one for me. If I was down, guys usually wouldn't keep hitting me, and if I had a guy down, I wouldn't hit him either."

The other thing that is hard for regular fans to understand is how two men can punch each other in the face—sometimes on multiple occasions—but still maintain some sort of a relationship. In fact, Barnaby admits that he actually became friends with opponents with whom he had serious issues on the ice. One in particular stands out.

"It is a little unusual that you would become friends with someone you had spent so much time trading punches with," Barnaby said. "Lyle Odelein is a guy that I hated more than anyone and fought him almost every time we played. We verbally jabbed each other and said nasty, nasty things to each other. Every time we played against each other I knew it was going to be a war. There were no easy nights for sure. After we retired, I knew many guys who had played with Odey, and they all told me what a great guy he was and what a great teammate he was. Guys told me we would have loved each other if we had played on the same team.

"I learned later of an incident where he almost lost his life. He was actually playing golf and he had one of those shooting cactuses hit his immune system and he was in very serious trouble. I found about it, and got his number, and I just wanted to reach out to him. I left him a message and just told him we had a lot of battles, but that I was hoping he was doing okay. I just told him I was thinking of him and his family.

"We ended up connecting, and he has even appeared on my podcast. When you do the job we do, you end up hating a lot of people and you fight a lot of people. But we also need to realize that we are all still just human beings. The guy on the other side is doing the exact same thing you are doing, but for his team. Once it's all over, and once the game is done, there are many guys that I've fought that I've had beers with, went to golf tournaments with, even vacationed with. Lyle seemed to be on the furthest end of the spectrum that the two of us could be, and we really hated each other for 15 years. Now I consider him a friend."

That is not to say Barnaby is friends with *everyone* he ever fought. In fact, the real animosity that existed between him and Sean Avery extended past their playing days. Not long ago, there were reports that Avery was going to sign with the Orlando Solar Bears of the East Coast Hockey League. That caused Barnaby to lobby other teams within the Solar Bears' division to sign him just so he could fight Avery again. There were also reports that legendary enforcer Georges Laraque also wanted to sign with a team just for the chance to beat up Avery one more time. Unfortunately for both Matthew and Georges, Avery's "tryout" lasted only two days and the Solar Bears announced they would not be signing him.

"I really did hate Sean Avery, but I've never actually met him," Barnaby said. "The difference between all of those other tough guys that I've got so much respect for and Sean is I've gotten to meet many of them. I also know others that they've played with and often they tell me what great guys many of them are. I've heard the complete opposite about Sean Avery. The stuff I've heard about how he treats trainers and equipment guys, and the way he's treated others, tells me I don't need to meet him to know the kind of person he is. It's been made crystal-clear to me many times. There is no need to meet him, but I would love to fight him. I'm still open to a charity match or even putting our own money on the line to fight him. But other than that, I have no need to meet that kind of guy."

Of course, while it's unusual in the real world, in professional hockey it is entirely possible that you end up playing *with* someone you had fought in the past or *against* a player you had been teammates and friends with. For hockey's enforcers, it is simply a part of the game.

"It is a little weird when you end up fighting a guy you've been friends with, especially when you fight a really tough guy that you've seen knock opponents out," Barnaby said. "You have an even greater appreciation for how tough they are. When you've got a tough teammate and he gets traded or signs somewhere else, you always think, 'Okay, this could happen. I might have to fight this guy.'

"Now, for the most part it doesn't, and often you have team-mates who might take on that friend for you. I'm talking about guys like Shawn Thornton, who I had been with in the Chicago Blackhawks organization, or a guy like Rob Ray, who I had din-ner with the night before we played in my first game back against the Sabres. Then you end up fighting this guy, and he's one of your best friends. Hey, things happen and there is always that possibility. You don't think about it until you or they get traded, and especially if you still play in the same division."

Barnaby played for seven teams in the NHL, so he had a lot of occasions to play with or against players he had tormented in the past. As is usually the case (but not always—see Archie Henderson and Willie Trognitz), a new friendship is formed or a previous relationship set aside for the 60 minutes you play against each other. Perhaps the most interesting situation for these players is stepping into a dressing room for the first time and meeting someone with whom they had developed a tumultuous relationship.

"I can honestly say that for the most part, it's always been great," Barnaby said. "A guy I hated the most was Eric Lindros, and I verbally tormented that guy for 10 years by the time I got to New York. And he ended up being my roommate! But when you're on the same team, and you both realize you're just doing that stuff for your teammates, you can overcome it pretty quickly.

"I can't speak for others, but for me it's always been a great experience to all of a sudden become teammates with someone you've battled with in the past. You get to know them, and I've always been someone who has been able to understand what we do for a living and how crazy it is. In almost every instance like that these guys have become very, very good friends."

Like every other NHL tough guy, Barnaby has paid a physical price for his profession. Most of them have no idea how many concussions they have experienced in the past and in most instances, they were not even diagnosed with one. Barnaby claims that he managed to avoid serious injury, although he can remember one time in particular when he was really tagged.

"I was never knocked out, but the hardest I've ever been hit was by Darren McCarty," Barnaby said. "I had been traded to Colorado and they had that heated rivalry with the Red Wings. I had never fought Mac before, but he hit me with a couple of lefts that really stung me bad. He broke my nose, I had cuts in my mouth, he split me right between my eyes and I was a mess.

"He cut me for 28 stitches, but I didn't really feel it yet, and Mac actually looked at me and said, 'Barns, you're leaking oil, man.' We both stopped and I felt the blood just dripping down my face. I got stitched up between periods and called home because I knew my kids were watching. I just wanted to make sure they knew I was okay. Darren McCarty hit me the hardest and cut me the worst, but he also stopped when he saw that I was hurt."

It's hard not to think about the toll making their living this way has taken on these men over a long period of time. In Matthew's case that means 13 NHL seasons and more than 800 NHL games—including nearly 200 NHL fights, plus countless others at the minor league and junior levels.

"I would be naive to not think about CTE and what could happen to me 20 years from now," Barnaby said. "We know so much more now than we ever did before and of course, you have to think about it. There is certainly the potential for so many guys who have been through so much physically. But do I live every day thinking about it or wishing I hadn't played the way I did? No! I had a choice about how I was going to make my living, and I did it. I don't regret anything, and I don't think about it on a daily basis. Now, does it creep up once in a while in conversation? Yeah, and I would have to be naive to think it may not have ramifications later on in my life."

There is currently no test available to diagnose the presence of CTE. Families of people who suffered from it can only learn of a definitive diagnosis posthumously. Many players in a number of sports have donated their brains for testing and diagnosis after their passing, in hopes of helping others in the future. While science is diligently working toward a diagnosis for living people, it still does not exist.

But that leads to the question I've asked several players for this book. If a test existed that could definitively tell a player he had CTE, would he want to take that test, knowing full well there is no treatment available?

"Ooh—that's a great question! Wow! I want to say no, because I just want to live my life and not worry all the time," Barnaby said. "Curiosity might get the best of me, and maybe I would wonder things like how long do I have and things like that. Maybe you could prepare better if you knew. But I kind of live life to the fullest as it is, so it's a really hard question. I'm really not sure of the answer to that one."

Now Barnaby has another perspective on the life of a hockey tough guy. His son, also named Matthew, has begun his professional hockey career. As this is being written, he is playing for the aforementioned Orlando Solar Bears of the ECHL. So what is it like for Matthew, who accumulated more than 2,500 NHL penalty minutes and had those 200 fights, to see his son playing the game at the professional level and knowing that he could be involved in fights of his own?

"It's 1,000 times harder!" Barnaby said. "Fortunately, that's not his game, and he's more of an offensive player. I think I was pretty progressive as a dad in my thinking and knowing how the game was going. I tried to teach him the complete opposite of how I played. I tried to teach him skills, and get that side of his game up to par. But any time he does fight, it's a lot harder to watch!

"I can't even comprehend what my mother, my brother, and my grandmother were going through when they watched me play the way I did. They watched me fight every single night, it seemed like. That is not fun for any parent."

Parenthood gave Matthew a different perspective on what it is like to watch someone you love involved in a bare-knuckle fistfight. But he came to that knowledge very late in the game.

"When I played I never realized it," Barnaby said. "I really took everything day by day—I didn't think about what happened the day before or what was going to happen tomorrow. It really wasn't until I retired and I saw my son playing that I realized how hard it was. You feel every hit, you see every fight, and it hurts you more than it does them. Those things didn't really hit me until I was done playing."

Matthew expresses almost no regrets for how he made his living and the way he played the game. It was a role he relished, was accomplished at doing, and was able to do for a long time. But that's not to say he has *no* regrets. Like everyone who does what he did for a living, there is at least one moment he would like to forget—or, more appropriately, wishes had never happened.

"There was one time in the minor leagues when I said something to a player about his brother, who had passed away. It's an emotional game, but if there was one thing I could take back it would be that. Things get said on both sides, back and forth, and sometimes you can cross the line, but this was one time when I was way out of bounds.

"After the game, I went to find the other player, and I apologized for my words. I was wrong. Everyone may have their own ideas of what's allowed and what isn't. I went over the line many, many, many, many times, but this was one time I went way over what was *my own* line. He was certainly not happy with me, and he had every right to feel that way, but he did accept my apology, and he seemed to be appreciative that I went down to seek him out, own up to what I did, and tell him I was sorry."

It might surprise people to learn that for some NHL tough guys, confrontation is often more verbal than physical. While he would like to take back that particular verbal shot, there are many others that he has given—and taken—that he can appreciate. Even when he is the recipient.

"The worst I ever got 'gotten' was in a game against Chris Simon," Barnaby said. "I had been ripping him about his family and where he came from, and he just responded with, 'Where's your dad?' Now, I didn't know my dad growing up, and I actually thought, 'Wow, that's a good one!' He didn't even swear or nothing! That was a like a mic drop moment. I was sitting in the penalty box thinking, 'How the hell does he know that?'

"We had the same agent, and I called my agent and asked him if he had told Chris about me. This was pre-internet, and there was no place he could have come up with it. My agent swore he never told him, and I never got to the bottom of it, but it was a damn good dig! A really good one!"

Who are the players in today's game that Matthew thinks have the best verbal dig game? One is a former teammate.

"I would say Steve Ott was really, really good at it," Barnaby said. "I was brought in to kind of mentor him as I was in the process of finishing my career. I tried to help him navigate through that crazy world by being a pest. He has some great one-liners! He was not afraid to rip every part of your family and your life."

In today's game, there is one undisputed king of the verbal game. Barnaby never played with or against Brad Marchand, but he certainly appreciates what Marchand can do.

"Brad Marchand is the best of the best when it comes to trash-talking," Barnaby said. "He is the double-edged sword. Not only can he trash-talk you and draw you into a penalty, but he's the one on the power play scoring the goal while you're in the box. He's the best, because he's such a great player too."

There are other similarities between Barnaby and Marchand. They are both players you could only appreciate if they were on your team—and both almost universally hated by opposing teams and their fan bases. When I tell people that Brad Marchand is a really fun guy to talk to and a great teammate, fans outside of Boston don't believe me. It was like that for Barnaby as well.

In the real world, Matthew Barnaby is not a small man. He played at 6'0" and 190 pounds. But in the universe of NHL tough guys, he was at best a light heavyweight and probably closer to a middleweight. Shawn Thornton was slightly larger than Matthew but has talked about always having to "punch up." They were almost always fighting men larger than themselves.

But in January 2001, Barnaby gamely took on way more than he could chew. He challenged a young 23-year-old defenseman for the New York Islanders. He goaded the 6'9", 250-pound Zdeno Chara to a fight—then held on for dear life. Not only did he fight Chara that night, the two fought on *three other* occasions. That begs the question—is fighting Chara courageous or just plain dumb?

"Every time we open up a bottle of wine and talk amongst friends, that same question comes up," Barnaby said. "Was it courageous or dumb? I would say the needle is someplace right down the middle of those two. It's a *little* courageous, but the more I think about it, it was probably dumb. You shouldn't go into a fight where you have *zero* chance to win. Against Zdeno I did that four times, and thankfully he's a really nice guy because it could have ended a lot worse. I've seen guys along the way who have fought him who ended up a lot worse than I did."

Barnaby's career ended in the 2006–07 season with the Dallas Stars. He played in only 39 games that season before retiring. How does he look back on a career that probably lasted longer than it should have, given his hockey beginnings?

"Look, part of me wishes I had 1,500 penalty minutes and 500 points," Barnaby said. "If I had fought a little less, I think I could have had more points, because I think I was a better player than 300 career points. But having said that, I'm really happy with the way my career played out. I would have loved to win a Stanley Cup, but that's not always in the cards for every player.

"I look back at the 300 points, and I guess it's an accomplishment. The 2,500 penalty minutes is a lot, and it means I showed up for a lot of games. The longevity I had, playing the role that I did, is probably the thing I'm most proud of. Numbers are just numbers, but hopefully everyone appreciates that I was a good teammate and I loved playing the game and battling hard."

CHAPTER 12

P.J. STOCK

<hr>

HERE'S THE THING about P.J. Stock—he is really funny. Laugh-out-loud, smart-ass, pain-in-the-rear-end funny. It serves him well in his post-career media work, but I'm not so sure it helped much when he was an undersized man playing the tough guy role in the National Hockey League. But Stock is the living, breathing embodiment of "his heart writes checks that his body can't cash." He just never believed that his body couldn't cash those checks.

Philip Joseph Stock was born in Dollard-des-Ormeaux, Quebec, in 1975 and never harbored any delusions of playing professional hockey. He knew at an early age that he was likely not big enough nor skilled enough to make his living playing the game. But he also had a goal from an early age to attend college in the United States.

"Growing up, we always watched Notre Dame football on the weekends, and we would sit around as a family on a Saturday," Stock said. "In the area that I grew up there were some of the older guys that I tried to emulate, and many of them went the college route. Kent Hughes went to Middlebury; his brother Ryan went to Cornell; Brad Purdy went to Maine; J.P. O'Connor went to Yale; and some other guys went to some pretty good schools too. Education was something that was important to me.

"I certainly never thought I would play a day of pro hockey. I wasn't drafted for any other reason except I was really s—t! I was really slow and not very good at 17 years old. I was even a defenseman back then. I had a couple of offers from schools in the States, but my parents didn't think I was mature enough to go. It's one thing being a couple of hours away, and it's another thing to be in a different country."

Stock was good enough to play two seasons for the Pembroke Lumber Kings of the Central Canada Hockey League. But it was his younger brother, Dean, who opened up the opportunity to play major junior hockey.

"My brother was playing midget AAA hockey at the time, and he was a pretty good hockey player," Stock said. "He already had representation and he was going to play major junior. But in Quebec, if you play a minute of major junior, you lose your college eligibility to get a scholarship. A couple of teams approached my brother and said they were willing to take him higher in the draft if I was willing to go play with him too. And they offered to pay for my education.

"My brother got drafted by Victoriaville, and I really liked the idea of playing with my brother, who was younger than me. I knew I was never gonna go on to anything in hockey, but I gave up on my United States university dream for the chance to play with him. We both made the team, and it was super cool to have that chance."

Stock became a defenseman for the Victoriaville Tigres of the Quebec Hockey League, and the penalty minutes started to pile up almost immediately. In his two seasons in Victoriaville, he had 384 and 432 penalty minutes. It didn't start because Stock was a fighter, but it ended up being that way.

"I was a defenseman who used to open-ice hit a lot," Stock said. "There was really not much fighting in the leagues before the Quebec League, but I got in a couple of fights that first year of Junior A, even though we were all wearing full cages. But now I go to Victoriaville and I'm still throwing those open-ice hits. So the other team would send a guy to beat me up.

"Mathieu Raby was my defense partner, and he was 6'4" and 225 pounds. He would save my ass every night! The problem is, back then, teams were a little deeper, and when Mathieu was in the penalty box they would just send another guy after me. I got beat up so many times that I figured I had to quickly learn to fight a little bit better and learn how to defend myself. I was a small guy who played that role, and it just kind of took off from there. A lot of guys wanted to beat me up—and they did!

"The tail end of my year-20 season in Victoriaville, we had a guy named Daniel Corso on our team who was a high draft pick of the St. Louis Blues. Back then the game was a little rougher, and by then I was the captain of the Tigres. Because Daniel was so good, teams would pick on him a bit, play him very physical. Our coach thought that because I was hardly ever back playing defense anyway, he would move me to forward to play with Daniel, maybe create a little space for him and let him play hockey.

That worked for a couple of games until we realized I was a s—t
forward too! So then they put me on a line with my brother and
we would match up with the other team's best lines. I was like a
third defenseman on the ice."

After Stock completed his junior eligibility, he was undrafted
with little or no professional prospects, so he enrolled at St. Francis Xavier University in Antigonish, Nova Scotia. He racked up
110 penalty minutes in just 27 games and surprisingly was offered
a tryout by the New York Rangers—an offer in which he was not
initially interested.

"I originally wasn't going to go, but then I figured why not?"
Stock said. "I went to the tryout, but I didn't know there was
a second gear. You were supposed to slow it down in training
camp, and the veterans don't go 100 percent. I was all over the
place, running everyone. I just missed Alexei Kovalev with an
open-ice hit and that's when Shane Churla and Ulf Samuelsson
both simultaneously ran me and threatened my life! This was all
new to me. I was never drafted, never been to a combine. I had
no idea how it all worked."

For reasons that Stock still finds baffling, the Rangers wanted
him to sign a contract and become a professional hockey player.
But their attempts to get him to sign felt a little bit like kidnap-
ping and extortion.

"At the end of camp, they cut all the guys they were sending
to the AHL, but I kind of stuck around a little bit longer," Stock
said. "Then the Rangers offered me a contract and wanted to send
me to the minors. I told them I wasn't going to sign and I was
going back to school.

"Now, this was the days before cell phones, and they put me in a room and closed the door. They told me they wanted me to sign the contract. I said, 'But I want to go to school! Where's my mom? I want to get out of here!'

"I left there without a contract, but then they approached me again. The exchange rate was 60 cents on the dollar at the time. The offer was the amount of a Canadian college education, which was $22,500, as a signing bonus, and I would only get it after my second year. I would get $18,000 in the ECHL, $30,000 in the AHL, and $300,000 in the NHL. I figured I would never see the American League or the NHL because guys I had grown up playing with couldn't make it, and they were better than me. I signed thinking it was worth $1.60 for $1.00 in Canadian money. I would play for a couple of years and come back with my Canadian university paid for.

"I ended up making the Hartford Wolfpack of the American Hockey League. I was about 185 pounds, playing forward, and every game I played I had to battle. I had 15 fights in my first nine games of pro hockey. Then 17 games into the season, the Rangers called me up. That's how it all started."

To hear it from Stock, he didn't belong in professional hockey. He described himself as slow, undersized, and not very good. But the Rangers saw enough to sign him to a contract and ultimately bring him up to the NHL. And Stock is pretty sure he knows why.

"I was good looking!" he said with a laugh. "No, I was just lucky. Right place, right time. It was a different time, and the game was played a certain way. I loved the physicality and the competitiveness. You'd have to ask the Rangers and find out why they kept me around.

"I went from chugging 25-cent beer and having the cheapest pizza I could find in college and six months later I'm sitting in a dressing room with Wayne Gretzky, Pat LaFontaine, Brian Leetch, and Mike Richter! My life changed pretty quickly."

As Stock said, he fought a lot to start his AHL career, and he had 202 penalty minutes in just 41 games in Hartford. That would be on pace for nearly 400 penalty minutes for an entire season. And while he was always undersized to play that kind of role, he says he didn't really mind doing it. Well, most of the time.

"I'm not gonna lie, I didn't mind it," Stock said. "The hardest part of the fighting was the thinking about it before. That was the part I didn't like. Obviously, I took some pretty good licks at times. Everything hurts the next day—your hands hurt, your neck hurts, you've got a fat lip, you can't eat anything normal. With all the cuts in your mouth, if you eat anything citrus or salty it really hurts. You can't wear your gloves properly because your knuckles are all cut up. It's hard to say I loved *that* part of it, and there were days when I hated it. But I also loved it.

"All of the rinks I played in I was either hated or I was really well liked. It was great to be noticed. I loved being the guy that no one liked. And I loved being the guy that people liked in their own building. It's a role, and there's a lot to learn. Luckily, I had some great players around me that I watched and tried to emulate.

"You end up learning on the job. I was really lucky and played with Darren Langdon at the start of my career, and I learned a lot just watching him. But I couldn't fight like him, because Darren was like 6'2" and weighed 210 pounds. But the wear and tear of taking a few to get one in takes a toll. A few broken bones here and there."

One of the things Stock had going for him was his ability to throw punches either with his left hand or his right. That skill kept him from losing a lot more than he did, despite his size.

"I switched hands all the time," Stock said. "Look, I was smaller than everyone and they usually outweighed me by 30 pounds. If they tried to hold me away, they could pretty much hold me out. I got punched in juniors one time pretty good and got hurt, and I never wanted it to happen again. I taught myself how to fight differently. Sometimes a good defense is a good offense, and I just wanted to keep this 6'3", 220-pound guy off balance for a few minutes. If he punched me once, I'm dead! I can't fight guys like that with my right against their right—they'll just hold me out and hammer me.

"I fought Steve McKenna one time and he was 6'8", 252 pounds. I was just waiting for him to throw a punch so I could grab an arm and hold on for dear life. Then I had to fight with whatever hand was free. If he's gonna hold my left, I'm gonna punch him with my right. It was a lot of adapt or die."

As his professional hockey career continued, Stock evolved and started to show more personality on the ice. But he almost feels like he was forced into it by his own teammates. They saw a guy every day who was different than the guy on the ice. They wanted him to show more of the personality they saw.

"I know I'm loud—at least, I'm like that in a locker room. But I'm not really that guy in real life," Stock said. "I like playing that way, but I'm not really like that. In juniors I knocked out the heavyweight of the league, Patrick Cote, who ended up playing for Nashville. He was a super tough guy. I got in a lucky punch. The guys on the team wanted me to pretend to put on the championship belt, but I just didn't do that! My teammates wouldn't let me get back on the bench.

"All I ever did was make fun of people who did stuff like that. Then, in my first fight in the American Hockey League—I don't know what I was thinking, or why I did what I did. I fought Mark Major [6'4", 216 pounds], and I don't know what came over me, but I kind of did the 'raise the roof' gesture. I didn't even win the fight! It's hard to explain to anyone who judges what happens in that moment, but the adrenaline rush that comes when you just survive a fistfight for your life is pretty crazy. This was one of those moments—and there were a couple during my career—that kind of just happened. I don't even know why they happened."

But it wasn't until P.J. signed with the Boston Bruins that something totally different happened—a move that quickly became known as the Wave. As Stock made his way to the penalty box after a fight, he began waving to the crowd.

"My first year with the Bruins, I was playing my first game back after an ankle sprain," Stock said. "We were playing a game in Buffalo in December, and I get in a fight down in the corner against Eric Boulton [6'1", 225 pounds], and he's a super tough guy. We went for quite a long time, and I had some cuts on my face, but I came out of it thankful I had survived. There was this open path down the middle of the ice going to the penalty box. The building was going nuts, and I got caught up in the moment and I did the wave.

"I don't think I ever fought selfishly. Maybe once or twice in my career I fought because I was frustrated, but I usually only fought because we were losing, the crowd was not in the game, trying to get some guy off our best player. Then the next time I fought, against Brad Ference, I thought had done pretty well in the fight, but no one in the building was even reacting, so I kind of half-assed did the wave and the place went nuts. Then I kind of had to f—ing do it every night!

"I would be bleeding, my head would be pounding, but the fans didn't care if I got the s—t kicked out of me or not; they wanted me to wave to them! So it just took off. I never wanted to be disrespectful to anyone; it was all about the fans and getting the building going and get the guys going. I know some people didn't love it, but I didn't really care what anyone else thought.

"I only cared about the guys on my team, and they knew why I was doing it. I had to find my niche, and I knew I was never going to be Joe Thornton or Glen Murray. I had to find a way to help the team be successful, and that's kind of what I fell into."

Do yourself a favor and pull up Stock's fight on January 5, 2002, on YouTube. The game was on national television for a Saturday matinee on ABC. Stock fought Steve Peat (6′2″, 235 pounds), and it was a *war*! Both guys stood toe-to-toe and just delivered punch after punch right to their opponent's face. By my rough count (and it was hard to keep up, with the speed punches were being delivered), Stock threw 36 punches and nearly all of them landed. Steve Levy, calling the game on ABC, said it was one of the best fights anyone had seen in a long time. As the linesman stepped in to break things up, Stock's and Peat's faces were already bleeding, and as Stock turned to go to the penalty box, he waved to the crowd. The roof blew off TD Garden, and Stock's "stock" went up even more. It even benefited him later in the night.

"That was one of the best bar nights of my life," Stock said. "It was awesome! Look, I was never drafted, and I was never in a place long enough to have a ton of success. I didn't have those moments of scoring the big goal or making the big play. I was never the hockey center of attention; I was just part of the group. That's why that night was so much fun for me. After the game, I was in a bar near the Garden and they kept showing the fight on the TVs in the bar and playing the song 'Kung Fu Fighting,' and they just kept doing it over and over again. I didn't have to pay for a beer that night!"

The "Stock Wave" went viral before that was even a thing. It even got picked up by at least one other player. The Bruins played the Ottawa Senators just two weeks after the Stock/Peat battle. After a Bruins goal, a line brawl broke out on the ice, and everyone had a dance partner. Senators goaltender Patrick Lalime got involved in the fight, so Boston goaltender Byron Dafoe came flying up the ice and squared off with Lalime.

Calling the Dafoe–Lalime fight was a highlight for me. I was working with former Bruins defenseman Gord Kluzak, and we were both laughing as Dafoe and Lalime were separated and skated to their respective benches. Lalime had a mouse over his left eye because Dafoe had clearly won the fight after both of their masks had been ripped off. There was a shot of Dafoe at the bench talking with Stock before Dafoe started laughing and gave his own weak attempt at the Stock Wave.

"I made him do it," Stock said. "I'm yelling at him, 'Do the wave! Do the wave!'"

Other NHL tough guys talk about Stock in almost reverent terms because of who he fought and how he fought. Shawn Thornton once told me Stock was willing to take a number of shots, just looking for a chance to land a big one of his own. It isn't recommended, but Stock seemed willing to do it that way.

"I fought Shawn a few times. He's an asshole," Stock said with a laugh. "He punched me like 15 times in a row in the head. He beat me up! He is such a strong man and did such a great job for Boston. I probably did take a few too many shots, but I just wasn't strong enough.

"In junior, I was an offensive defenseman, and I was pretty good on defense. My number is retired there! I go to college and become a center, and there's no fighting there. Then the fighting thing just kind of took off when I turned pro. I had those 15 fights in my first nine pro games, and I didn't look for one of them. They just kind of happened."

Stock only played two seasons for the Boston Bruins, and his last game was in 2003, but to this day Bruins fans speak of him with love. If you attend a game at TD Garden even now, you are likely so see someone wearing a bootleg black T-shirt with No. 42 on the back, P.J. STOCK above the number, and Ass KICKER below it.

"Cops came into the Garden one night and brought a box of T-shirts that said P.J. STOCK Ass KICKER on the back," Stock said. "They told me there were people selling these shirts outside the building with my name on them and asked if I wanted them to confiscate the shirts. I said, 'Are you kidding me? This is the best thing ever! Let me buy a bunch!' I said they could sell them as long as they gave me some. It was awesome!"

It's hard for Stock to understand his impact on Bruins fans, but ultimately it comes down to being a lot like the people sitting in the stands chanting his name.

"The cities I played in were really blue-collar cities," Stock said. "Say what you want about Boston, but Bruins fans were all blue-collar. All they wanted was an honest effort—'I don't care what you do, just go kick their ass!' That's why I loved playing there. I was part of the St. Patrick's Day parade in Southie. I think Boston fans thought I was one of them, and I felt like I was one of them too. Fans probably thought I could barely do a crossover, but I was willing to fight for my team and my city."

Matthew Barnaby says a lot of the job of an NHL tough guy involves trash-talking. You say almost anything to get your opponent off his game or goad him into taking a penalty against you that gives your team an advantage. But Stock says that was a weak part of his game, despite his sense of humor and ability to talk.

"When you're 5'10", 185 pounds, it's hard to say much of anything because then you have to back it up," Stock said. "I had my one-liners, but they didn't really go that well. Someone would hit Sergei Samsonov and I would yell, 'You do that again and I'm gonna kick your ass!' They would usually just look at me and say, 'Shut up, short stuff!' I couldn't really say anything. So, I would go threaten their better player—like, I would tell Joe Sakic, 'Hey, if Jeff Odgers takes one more run at Sergei, I'm coming after you!' Then Sakic would tell me to shut up too! I had to just go out on the ice and get guys riled up enough that they wanted to beat me up."

Stock is bitter about how his career in Boston came to an end. He was signed to a two-year contract by general manager Mike O'Connell but almost immediately shipped to the minors. The team started the season on a road trip and Stock traveled to Florida with them. A day later, he left because he had been assigned to Providence of the American Hockey League. He only played four games in Providence—somewhat lackluster, by his own admission, because he didn't understand why the Bruins had given up on him—and then O'Connell assigned him to the Philadelphia Phantoms of the AHL.

"Within the first week I was in Philly, I hurt my orbital bone again," Stock said. "I was under contract to the Bruins, but they never reached out to me again. I had to wear a cage for a number of weeks, and the first day I take it off I get a stick to my eye. I was pretty much done at that point.

"The Bruins didn't really believe I was hurt. During the lockout year, I saw doctors for the entire year. The team made me show up every morning at the rink, check in, and do a workout every day. They were trying to get me to quit. I ended up having the surgery and it caused double vision. I have double vision even now, and that's why I stopped playing."

Just like that, Stock's professional hockey career was over. He couldn't play because of the double vision, but his urge to compete continues to this day.

"Your body can only take so much of a beating, but I'm dumb and I just keep doing things," Stock said. "I play rugby still against guys who are like 22 to 25 years old, and I'm 47! It's just that rush. It's that physical mentality that I can still do it. In that role, and in life, you can never really lose it. I just always want to compete to your highest level.

"I'm better off than almost all of the guys who made a living the way I did. Near the end of my career, my energy level was getting low. Maybe I could have used a little longer break from time to time, maybe my body and my head needed more time to recover. But I knew I couldn't have continued like that for another 10 years. I had a good run. I'm very fortunate. I got out of a very physical game and all I had was a few bumps and bruises. I'm very lucky."

He has gone on to a busy post-playing career. His personality and ability to talk made him a natural fit for the media business, and he made the transition smoothly. He had his own radio show and was an analyst on *Hockey Night in Canada*. His position, along with several others, was an economic casualty when Rogers Media overreached with their new *Hockey Night in Canada* package and suffered large losses. He is bilingual and continues to work in television and hockey analysis.

Believe it or not, P.J. Stock has another title—figure skater. He got the call to participate on CBC's reality series *Battle of the Blades*, where he competed against Russian Violetta Afanasieva.

"Hey, man, adapt or die!" Stock said with a laugh. "That show is the Canadian version of *Dancing with the Stars*. I competed on it one year, then I got a call asking me to be a judge on the show. Then a couple of years ago a guy got hurt, and the producers thought, 'Who is dumb enough that we can call and after two weeks of no practice, put on figure skates and go stand at center ice on national television?' They made one call!

"I've been so lucky in my post-playing career. I've worked the Olympics, I do TV up in Canada, I do media work and my podcast. I worked as a sports marketer for a communications company. I've been very, very, very fortunate. For a career that wasn't that long, and probably not that great, I get some great opportunities. I tell people, the only thing you've got to do is just be remembered. Just be remembered. I'm grateful that people still remember me."

Stock can even sound a bit philosophical when he looks back on his professional hockey career and how suddenly it ended.

"When you play, you go through a lot," he said. "My career ended and there were so many people that I played with that I wish I could have said goodbye to and thank you. Everyone that you play with influences your life, positively or negatively. There's so many guys, and there's a lesson to be learned every day. I didn't realize it, but now that I'm a dad and have kids and have been blessed to do lots of other things, I get it. You try to emulate people that you listen to in life. I like to go back and watch YouTube—maybe not figure skating—and relive some of those nice moments."

The way Stock looks at life used to be able to be summed up in one phrase he used to say all the time: "Everything happens for a reason." But he stopped saying that when his brother, Dean, passed away from ALS in 2016.

"I used to say everything happens for a reason until Dean died. Then I didn't believe that was true," Stock said. "His death changed everything. Anyone who tells you something like that doesn't change you is completely wrong. It changes how you look at everything. You become a lot more understanding to a lot of people in life. It opens up your heart more than it ever was before. It's no longer the glass is half-full or the glass is half-empty—just be proud you have a glass.

"My brother was a better hockey player than I was, but some guys make it and some guys don't. He played for a few years on the coast, then ended up not making it. He was one of my biggest supporters. He would come to Boston, and he was the first guy wanting to buy one of the Ass Kicker T-shirts. For Halloween he dressed up as me. We had a great relationship. In The Greatest Bar in Boston, they have a corner with pictures of a bunch of tough guys. We have a great photo of my brother wearing my shirt, sitting under my picture."

Stock's time in Boston didn't last long, but his impact can be felt even today. Ask any Bruins fan which tough guys they remember, and his name invariably comes up. He may not understand it completely, but Bruins fans do. You love who you love.

CHAPTER 13

BOBBY ROBINS

YOU'D BE FORGIVEN if you don't know Bobby Robins. If you didn't grow up in Peshtigo, Wisconsin, or follow the University of Massachusetts–Lowell and Providence Bruins as a fan, Robins' hockey career might have eluded you. After all, he only played a total of three games in the National Hockey League. But I can honestly say that of all the people I spoke to for this book, Bobby's story may have had the biggest impact on me.

Robins' mom, Adelina, moved from her native Philippines when she was 19 years old to go to college in Northern Wisconsin. It was there that she met Rod Robins. They fell in love and got married, then had a daughter named Jennifer and, five years later, a son named Bobby.

You can be a pretty big fish in a pretty small hockey pond in Peshtigo, so Robins had to move around a bit in pursuit of his hockey dreams.

"I started climbing the hockey ranks when I was young and ended up moving from our small town of Peshtigo to playing youth hockey in Green Bay," Robins said. "Then in high school I left home and went to Culver Military Academy. After that I went to a bunch of tryouts and got cut from a bunch of teams, and that's when I learned about the fighting aspect of the game.

"I ended up making a team out in Montana, and had a good year there that led to the USHL. After I had another good year there too, I ended up going to UMass–Lowell. I had never even heard about Lowell, but after I started putting up points in the USHL I got a call from the coach, Blaise McDonald, and got the chance to go there."

As Robins said, he had begun to find out about the fighting aspects of hockey playing first for the Great Falls Americans in the American West Hockey League, and continuing while playing for the Tri-City Storm in the United States Hockey League. But to jump from the USHL to Hockey East meant fighting was no longer part of his game—and he welcomed that.

"In college, I was able to be a very physical player, a very heavy forechecker, and a guy who was always pushing and shoving in every scrum after whistles," Robins said. "I just played with a lot of snarl. Fear was always a big factor for me in the fighting game. I was always afraid before every game because of that aspect of the game. But in college, I knew I didn't have to fight because you aren't allowed to, so I didn't have that same fear. That allowed me to play a pure brand of hockey without those fearful thoughts in the back of my head.

"I had 94 penalty [minutes] in 35 games my last year at Lowell, and that's a lot of penalty minutes, but I got a lot of those just from checking. I would just run a guy through the glass and get a five-minute checking from behind penalty. Blaise would tell me,

'Bobby, those aren't penalties in the NHL. We call those checking-too-hard penalties.' Sometimes getting called for those was very frustrating, but I kept getting encouragement that if I just played the same way when I got to the pros those would just be good hard hits."

Robins wasn't the first tough guy I've talked to who admitted to being afraid of fighting. Fear can take many forms, and more than one player expressed, primarily, a fear of letting teammates down. Another common fear was being embarrassed. Few players ever admitted to being afraid of getting hurt. They all talk about going into a zone of sorts, and physical pain is not on their minds. It may well be an outcome of fighting, but they generally don't fear it or even acknowledge it. Almost without exception, tough guys are afraid of losing a fight (and the adverse effect it can have on their team) or letting their teammates down. Tough guys also feel like they can never afford to have an off night. If a goal scorer has an off night, he doesn't score and tries to make up for it in the next game. If a tough guy has an off night, his entire team can be affected, and he can end up getting himself or someone else hurt.

Robins had been scouted his senior year at Lowell by Peter Chiarelli of the Ottawa Senators. After he played his final college game, Chiarelli offered Robins a 25-game Pro Tryout Agreement (PTO) to play for Binghamton Senators. He played in 16 games and had seven points to go along with 19 penalty minutes. But the jump from the college game to the professional ranks brought with it a return to his anxiety.

"When I started playing in the American Hockey League, the fear factor was back in a very big way," Robins said. "I was arguably the heavyweight champ of the USHL before UMass–Lowell, and I was a really good fighter at that level. But after four years of college hockey with almost no fighting, I forgot how to do that part of the game, and I especially forgot the fear factor. I knew I was going to have to do it again in Binghamton, and I just played as hard as I could, hitting everything in sight. When I started, because of the way I was playing, not many guys were asking me to fight, except the real big heavyweights. The veterans on my team would tell me, 'Yeah, don't fight *that* guy. Leave him on the ice.' So I would say no to those guys, and I didn't get challenged that often.

"Then I had one big fight with Jamie Pushor that became kind of legendary against a legendary tough guy over his career in the AHL. I ended up kind of beating him up and doing a good job in that fight, so I earned a little bit of a reputation that I could fight. But I certainly didn't do it to the extent that I did at the end of my career. I would get maybe six to eight fighting majors a season my first couple of years of pro, and for a guy like me that just wasn't enough. It wasn't until I made a conscious decision to make that a consistent part of my game that it really took off."

Talk to Robins for any length of time and you are struck immediately by his honesty and his willingness to be introspective. That self-assessment is certainly a more recent development in his life—more on that later. But he's even willing to discuss the topic considered taboo for many tough guys who often won't even acknowledge being afraid, let alone try to figure out *why* they were afraid.

"Man, I've been asking myself this question for quite a while now," Robins said. "I think it's mainly the fear of losing and the fear of embarrassment. When you're fighting another man in hand-to-hand combat, that's as real and as raw as it gets. It gives you a glimpse of your guts and who you really are. I got a glimpse of myself, and I was really a coward. I was afraid to do it, and that ate me up for a lot of years. But I always did it because I was made to do it, and maybe it was my destiny. I was always a tough kid, and I could always fight and handle myself. It wasn't until I accepted that that was what I was going to do that I was able to handle the fear. But the fear was always there, and my first couple of years it really got to me. I didn't fight the way I should have playing on an NHL contract. Looking back on it, I have a lot of regret. I wish I had played in that first contract the way I was in Boston and Providence."

Like many NHL tough guys, Robins can find himself in front of his computer screen for hours watching fights and studying fighters.

"Sometimes I stay up late at night and get sucked into watching a bunch of old hockey fights on YouTube," Robins said. "A hockey fight is an amazing thing to see, especially when you're in one. As I said, I always had a lot of fear building up to it, but when the gloves were finally off, I often felt like I was in my element. It felt like a natural place and that's where I was supposed to be. I loved that aspect of it. I really enjoyed watching it afterward, and it was like breaking down film. Sometimes it surprised me that it was actually me out there doing it. I never hated doing it, but there was just that fear. Once I accepted it, I went into every game as if it were a war zone. There is some stress that comes with that, but I really loved the war zone and the battle. I wanted to be that guy who was there to protect my teammates. There was a lot of honor in that."

Like I told John Shannon, I pointed out to Robins that the most brittle bones in the human body are the small bones in the hand and that the hardest bones in the body are many of the large bones composing the skull and forehead area. That means it probably makes little sense to punch another human being in the face and head—or worse, on a hard plastic helmet—with your bare knuckles.

"Wow, isn't that something? It used to be that you would take off your bucket—drop the gloves and the buckets. Now guys keep their helmet on. The way you say it, it certainly sounds like a silly thing, but sometimes in a hockey game it seems like the most organic thing to happen. It just breaks out! There is something beautiful about a hockey fight that doesn't really exist anywhere else.

"I never broke any bones in my hand—I guess I was lucky. But I did sever a tendon when I knocked a guy's teeth out once."

After an 80-game season with Binghamton in his second professional season, Robins began the vagabond existence of the hockey journeyman. He spent a season playing in Elmira, Rochester, Albany, and Syracuse with few results to show. It appeared that his North American hockey career was over, and he tried his hand at playing in Europe. He spent a season with the Belfast Giants of the British Elite Ice Hockey League, and he even had good numbers, albeit in a league several rungs below the AHL.

The next season, he moved on to the Austrian League and a season with Jesenice. That experience finally caused Robins to reassess his place in life and his career goals. He spent a lot of the season sitting on the bench and had just three goals and four assists in 34 games to go along with 178 penalty minutes. It was rock bottom.

"I think I only fought twice that entire season," Robins said. "A lot of those penalty minutes were just from checking. I hit a guy so hard one time that I got suspended for five games, just for a massive open-ice body check, a *clean* check! So a lot of those penalty minutes were those 'checking too hard' penalties.

"I was certainly in the wrong league, that's for sure. That was the moment for me. I was sitting on the bench, not getting any points and not really playing. I couldn't figure out what they wanted. Did they want me to be a goon? Did they hire me to just come here and fight guys? That was when I decided to rededicate myself and make a real legitimate run for the NHL. That summer was my all-out effort to make it professionally over here. It was a simple story—make it here, or finally give up my dream."

With his career hanging by a thread and his life in shambles, Robins had other issues he had to confront, including a longtime battle with addiction. Unfortunately, it was only his first battle against substances, not his last.

"I almost gave up, after that fourth year of pro," Robins said. "I was in Austria, riding the pines and not playing. I had no contract offers and really everything in my life fell apart. I was addicted to chewing tobacco for over a decade, and I had a growth in my mouth that they biopsied to see if I had cancer. That was the catalyst for me to quit that addiction. I was hopelessly addicted to it.

"That summer when all of this was happening, I was dating this girl, who is now my wife. I knew I wanted to marry

her and provide for her. It caused me to look at my life with
so much regret because I felt I had failed in my goal to play in
the National Hockey League. I had a lot of regret and a lot of
resentment. I decided that if I could quit chewing tobacco, then
I could accomplish my other career goals. That's when the dream
came back alive for me. I decided to do it right and got in the
best shape of my life. I also committed to learning how to fight
and decided to fight 20 to 30 times a year—40 one year! It was
a pivotal moment in my life."

For Bobby Robins, "doing it right" and "rededicating his
efforts" really meant just one thing—fighting. He felt, given his
skill set, it was his only avenue to playing professional hockey. So
that meant a conscious decision to fight 20 to 30 times a year or
more. First, he returned to North American professional hockey
with the Bakersfield Condors of the ACHL. There were also stops
with the Chicago Express of the ECHL and the Abbotsford Heat
of the AHL. Then came the call he had been waiting for.

"Peter Chiarelli never forgot me. He originally signed me out
of Lowell when he was with Ottawa, and now when he was with
the Bruins, he wanted to give me a chance to play for the Providence Bruins in the AHL. He gave me a second chance to do it
right. I went in there and tried to play the way Peter wanted me
to play when he first signed me. I finally became that player."

Robins and his wife had a game plan, and a big part of that
plan involved Bobby being willing to address his fears and fighting for a living.

"No one believed in me except for me and my wife, Samantha.
We made an agreement that we were going to give it two years,
and if I didn't get a chance to at least make a real living in the

American League, that was going to be it. All of a sudden, I got the call just after Christmas when I playing in the East Coast League to come to Providence. They told me to come for a week, and then they put me in an apartment and I signed for the rest of the year.

"All of these little steps kept coming together after many, many nights of visualizing what it could be like. After the lockout season, I signed a two-year deal with Boston and I saw myself climbing the ranks and becoming a legitimate name in the sport. I started to sense that even at my age, maybe I *could* play in the NHL."

A look at what Robins put himself through in three years in Providence was an indication of what he was willing to do. In his first year there, that meant 150 penalty minutes in 33 games. In his second full season, the numbers amped up dramatically and he had 316 penalty minutes in 74 games. The next year Robins picked up another 221 penalty minutes in 68 games.

"It was really neat to go from four years of hockey at UMass–Lowell to moving right down the road to play in Providence," Robins said. "There is something about New England, and hockey fans really appreciate that blue-collar work ethic. Lowell was the hometown for Irish Mickey Ward. I really came into my own as a hockey player and earned some notoriety.

"I really made my comeback in Providence. I became a legitimate pro hockey player there. I was in my thirties and playing a regular shift in the American Hockey League, and I felt better than I did when I was in my twenties. I hit everything I could, and those fans at The Dunk [Dunkin' Donuts Center, now named Amica Mutual Pavilion] really embraced me and I embraced them.

"One of the greatest honors I ever had was being named to the All-Time Providence Bruins team in 2020. I looked at that roster, with names like Patrice Bergeron, David Krejci, David Pastrnak, and Tuukka Rask—some really big names on there—and somehow the fans selected me to be on that list too. I really loved getting that place rocking on a Saturday night."

Those three seasons in Providence didn't just earn Robins a spot on the Providence All-Time team. They earned him a chance to fulfill his dream and play in the National Hockey League.

When the Boston Bruins opened the 2014–15 season, they did so with a man making NHL history: at the age of 32, Bobby Robins was the oldest rookie in league history to make an opening day roster. After playing for seven teams in four different leagues, in North America and in Europe, Robins had made it.

"Standing there for the national anthem was a pretty amazing feeling," Robins said. "After five years of really hard work, playing all over the place, and giving every ounce of me, I was finally there."

Robins also knew he would absolutely be fighting someone from the opposing Philadelphia Flyers. It was just a question of who.

"When I made my NHL debut I knew, for sure, I was going to have a fight against someone on the Flyers," Robins said. "I always look at the rosters, and I saw Zac Rinaldo's name on there. He was really well known, and I had seen all of his fights. I knew his M.O., and I knew he threw those big arching bombs, and had legitimate knockout power. I also knew that Luke Schenn was a big lefty. If you're in my line of work, you know the strategy of every opponent and if they threw lefty or righty. Those two were on my list, but I was a little nervous about Rinaldo. I got smoked by Rinaldo in my first shift and that rang my bell. Then I had the fight with Schenn."

It's hard to say, looking back on it, what began the inevitable descent from there. Was it the hit from Rinaldo? Was it the fight with Schenn? While Robins doesn't necessarily know the answer himself, he does know that things got worse from there.

"The next night in Detroit, I took two more shots up high in my head," Robins said. "Then in the game against Washington, I took one final blow to the head. Michael Latta came in and hit me in my chin and we fought, and everything kind of went blank after that."

After three games in the NHL, the Bruins placed Robins on waivers to send him back to Providence. His dream was over, but his nightmare was just beginning.

"The feeling was disappointment, letdown, and failure," Robins said. "By then I was really struggling with concussion issues and was trying to play through it. For me, there was a lot of confusion. I think my brain was already shifting into a dark and depressive state. The news that I was getting sent down certainly didn't help with that. It all kind of snowballed from there.

"When they told me they were sending me down, I knew I had two days to clear waivers, and I wasn't feeling right and I just wanted to try and sleep it off, so that's what I did. But it didn't go away after that.

"After two days to clear waivers, I went down to Providence and played in the two games over the weekend. I didn't really do anything, and every day the headaches kept getting worse and worse. After the two games I finally said something to the training staff and told them I had a concussion."

At that point, Robins didn't know what he didn't know. He wasn't alone. Many players, in many different sports played through much more than they would be allowed to today. We've learned a lot about concussions and CTE, and Bobby was just beginning his education.

"A lot of information has come out since then about multiple head traumas," Robins said. "If you get hit once, it does some damage—if you get hit twice, it does even more damage and there is a compound effect. I had made the NHL, and even though I got my head dinged in that first game, I made the decision I was just going to play through it. There was nothing that was going to stop me. I was literally ready to die in order to chase that dream.

"After working with a lot of amazing doctors over the past several years, I've learned about that phrase, 'getting your bell rung.' How many times did I 'get my bell rung' in a game or in a fight and just play through it? Now we know that those are concussions and they are doing damage to your brain. For me, there was just that one time when the symptoms wouldn't go away, but I've had my fair share of times when I 'got turned off' or knocked out for a split second, and those are all concussive blows. They're all doing something to your brain as well."

There have been other NHL players in recent memory who have fallen victim to concussions, head trauma, and perhaps burgeoning CTE. Bob Probert died on July 5, 2010, at the age of 45. He is the fifth-most-penalized player in NHL history with 3,300 career penalty minutes. He suffered a heart attack while boating on Lake St. Clair and, despite efforts to revive him, was pronounced dead that afternoon. Probert's family donated his brain to the Sports Legacy Institute and researchers at Boston University found evidence of CTE.

Derek Boogaard died on May 13, 2011, at the age of 28. While recovering from a concussion, he fell victim to an accidental drug and alcohol overdose. Boogaard had a long history of battling drug and alcohol abuse and had been in rehab on several occasions. A study of his brain also found CTE at even greater levels than Probert's. Boogaard's parents unsuccessfully sued the National Hockey League Players Association, seeking nearly $10 million in damages. In 2013, the suit was dismissed when the judge ruled the Boogaards had waited too long to make the claim.

Just months after Boogaard's death, Rick Rypien and Wade Belak also passed away with similar medical issues to those plaguing Probert and Boogaard. Rypien had reportedly suffered from depression for more than 10 years when he committed suicide at the age of 27. He was diagnosed with CTE.

Belak died on August 31, 2011, at the age of 35. Toronto police initially treated the death as a suicide, but it was ultimately ruled an accidental death. Belak was yet another former player who was diagnosed posthumously with CTE.

Robins, like so many tough guys in professional hockey, was also the victim of simple physics. He was a middleweight playing a heavyweight's game, and the cumulative effective was taking a toll. He knew it but was still willing to accept the outcome.

"When I was in my best shape, I was 6'1" and 215 pounds—pretty lean," Robins said. "The way the NHL went after the lockout, guys like me became those fourth-line, checker-fighter kind of players. I considered myself kind of a mid-heavyweight, and

I had to fight some of the legitimate heavyweights and could do okay, but never considered myself a true heavyweight. Later on, I got lumped into the group with those bigger guys just because I was fighting so much. Shawn Thornton told me, 'Guys like us always have to fight up and fight guys bigger than us.' We were fighting guys who were in that 6'4", 230- or 240-pound range. Those are some big boys!"

Those two games in Providence were the last two hockey games Robins ever played. His career was over, a victim of concussions, head trauma, and the cumulative effect of a physical life on the edge. Robins has spent a large portion of his post-hockey life trying to get his life and health in order. He rediscovered his faith in God and spends a lot of time speaking to youth groups as part of the Christian Sports Ministry.

"I wasn't a believer during my hockey career—that came after my career ended," Robins said. "I had some tough struggles with post-concussion syndrome, depression, drug and alcohol abuse, thoughts of suicide. I was really in a rough spot at the end of my hockey career. That caused me to take a bigger picture look at my life.

"I was brought up in a Christian church as a kid but rejected that as a young man. But when I was at my lowest, I picked up a Bible and responded to the gospel for the first time in my life in 2016. I became a man of faith. I'm definitely not perfect—only one man ever was. But trying to live that every day is an important part of my life."

There's that famous Bobby Robins honesty. He shares with young people his struggles with substance abuse, depression, and even suicidal ideation. He admits he is probably lucky to even be here talking about all of this today. And it was this part of our conversation that really got me thinking about fighting, the price paid by hockey enforcers, and how much I really wanted to see it continue in the sport. When Robins told me he'd had thoughts of suicide, it really brought me up short and left me a little breathless.

"It got closer than just thoughts—let's just say that," Robins said. "There were times when I was holding a gun in my hand and pondering what would happen if I just ended it. There were other times when I was just really reckless, driving too fast and burning through stop signs with no thoughts of the consequences.

"On a couple of occasions, it got closer than just thinking about it, and at the darkest it became a thing I couldn't stop focusing on. I was thinking of suicide and even planning, but thank God it never got that far. I look back on it and think I'm really lucky to even be alive. Hopefully, I'm still here for a reason."

So, how does a man who speaks glowingly about his loving relationship with God reconcile that love with his previous profession of bare-knuckle brawling? Robins told me about how fighting was an almost beautiful thing. Does that fit in with his religious faith?

"The most famous fight, in the history of fights, was in the Bible," Robins said. "It involved a boy named David, and he fought a giant named Goliath. If my belief is true that God wrote the Bible, and it was inspired by God, then it sounds like he's a fan of a good fight! David won the fight and became the king. I always thought of myself as that underdog fighting these big giants. I was also a man on a mission with a destiny to chase. It sounds like God likes fighters!"

Robins readily admits he doesn't know what the future will bring. He also knows that his past is something that could catch up with him, and he is well aware of the dangers.

"I've spent a lot of time looking into CTE and really being concerned for myself too," Robins said. "I've been in a lot of fights, but even more than that I was always a very violent checker. I always played with significant impact on my body. Throughout my career, I always thought I just had a really hard head, and that I was just tougher than everyone else and would never get hurt. Then when it did happen, and I saw myself decline very quickly through depression, drug and alcohol abuse, and thoughts of suicide, I started to wonder if CTE was happening to me. I don't have the answer to that. I sure hope not. But I still struggle with impulse control and anger issues. I don't think I'm out of the woods yet. I'm still a work in progress, trying to get better every day.

"It's strange to think there may be this degenerative disease, and it may be inside my body right now, but I've made a decision to not think about it or dwell on it. I'm going to be the best version of me that I can be and as a man of faith I know everything is in God's hands."

In autopsies, many athletes' brains have shown evidence of CTE. It is expected that a test will be developed sometime in the near future that will allow a diagnosis in living people. I've asked several players if they would take the test today if medical science made it available.

"That's a good question," Robins said. "I don't know. I'm not sure if I would want to know I had CTE. I think I might not want to know. If I had the option, I would not take the test."

I have to admit that as Robins answered my question, it again got me thinking. Would I want to know if I had a debilitating medical condition, with no known cure and no known time frame? Would I want to know I was on the road to a steep physical decline but couldn't do anything about it? It's like that old question about whether you would want to know when you were going to die. It seems logical to believe that knowledge would adversely affect whatever time you have remaining.

As he continues his journey to self-awareness, Robins has laid his soul bare in an as-yet-unpublished autobiography. It's another confirmation of Robins' honesty and self-effacement that the original title was *Meat Stick*. That was how Bobby saw himself as a hockey enforcer with a willingness to put his health and well-being at risk. He has since changed the name of his autobiography to *Sex, Drugs, Pucks, and Souls*.

The autobiography is searingly honest and deals with some subjects that are difficult to talk about. Robins has even expressed some concerns about his own children reading it when they get a little older and how he will deal with it when that time comes. But, as always, he deals with things head-on, and says he'll do the same with his children. He'll be honest and acknowledge that he is not the same man now that he was in an earlier part of his life.

At the end of our last talk, I asked Robins a simple question: "What does Bobby Robins want to be when he grows up?" His answer, as always, was honest and to the point.

"Bobby Robins wants to be a famous and notable writer and author. Maybe not famous, but at least impactful."

I wouldn't bet against him.

ACKNOWLEDGMENTS

T HERE ARE SO MANY PEOPLE to thank now that I've finished my third book.

I start with Bill Ames at Triumph Books, who gave me the opportunity to write my first book back in 2018 with *If These Walls Could Talk: Boston Bruins*. He then afforded me the chance to coauthor *Shawn Thornton: Fighting My Way to the Top* in 2021. I came to Bill with an idea for this project, and he expressed enthusiasm for it immediately. I hope to continue to earn that trust.

Michelle Bruton has served as my more-than-able editor and sounding board for all three projects, and although we've never met in person, I consider her a dear friend.

My thanks to all the people in this book who trusted me to tell their stories—Terry O'Reilly, Dave Brown, Archie Henderson, Chris Nilan, Jay Miller, Paul Stewart, Bobby Robins, Milan Lucic, Matthew Barnaby, P.J. Stock, Brian Burke, John Shannon, and

Mike Milbury. I am eternally grateful for their willingness to participate, and I hope people enjoy their stories. My thanks also to others who participated in supporting roles—people like Don Cherry, Jamie Huscroft, and Harry Sinden.

I could not complete a project like this without the continuing love and support of my family—my wife, Susan; Taylor and Lauren; Alysha, Carolyn, and Parker; and Brianna and Bradley. They help build my confidence, even when I have my own serious self-confidence issues, and I love them all.

I also acknowledge that this project didn't end the way it began. I have had some increasing doubts about the effect of fighting on the men who played the game that way, and talking with these men did nothing to calm them. I'm thrilled that most of these guys seem to be okay and have virtually no regrets about their career paths. But I also implore the National Hockey League and the people who run it to continue to explore the long-term effects of concussions, head trauma, and CTE.

Thank you, finally, to the people who read my works. It means more than you will ever know.

FURTHER READING

Books by the *Tough Guys*

Barnaby, Matthew, with Kevin Shea. *Matthew Barnaby: Unfiltered*. Chicago: Triumph Books, 2022.

Nilan, Chris. *Fighting Back: The Chris Nilan Story*. Chicago: Triumph Books, 2013.

Thornton, Shawn, with Dale Arnold. *Shawn Thornton: Fighting My Way to the Top*. Chicago: Triumph Books, 2021.

Also by Dale Arnold

If These Walls Could Talk: Boston Bruins: Stories from the Boston Bruins Ice, Locker Room, and Press Box. Chicago: Triumph Books, 2018.